Make And Sell Digital Travel Photos

Take the Mystery Out Of Having Your Travel Photos Published

David Hilbert

Published By SST Publications
8987 E Tanque Verde # 309-377
Tucson, AZ 85749

ISBN # 978-0-9816713-3-8
0-9816713-3-0

Printed in the United States of America

Acknowledgements
Thanks to photographers Rain Rodolph and Jeanne McKenna for the use of their photos and for their collaboration on many travel and trade assignments.

Thanks to Joseph Beazely, Professor Hector Palacios Flores, Stephano McGhee, and Glen Pollack, for advice on editorial content.

Cover Photo: David Hilbert
AP 14

In 1519, Leonardo da Vinci described the use of the Camera Obscura to aid in drawing. The principle would later lead to the first photograph.

Make And Sell Digital Travel Photos

Take the Mystery Out Of Having Your Travel Photos Published

David Hilbert

Photos by Rain Rodolph, Jeanne McKenna, and David Hilbert

Photos that you make while on vacation can sell.

Take a little time and care in making your travel photos and they can help pay for your travel vacation.

Learn how to create digital photos that editors will buy.

Learn how to present proposals to an editor.

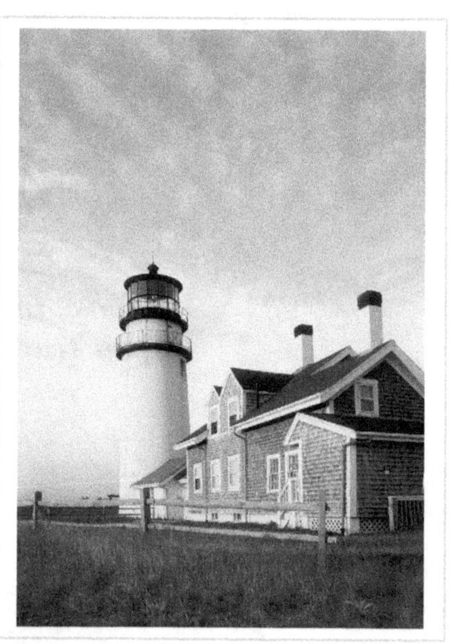

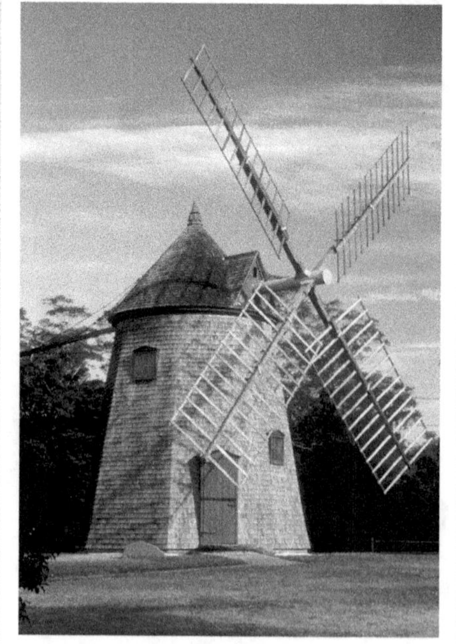

See Part One for techniques that you will need to make marketable photos.

See Part Two for tips on how to present your photos to an editor for consideration in a publication.

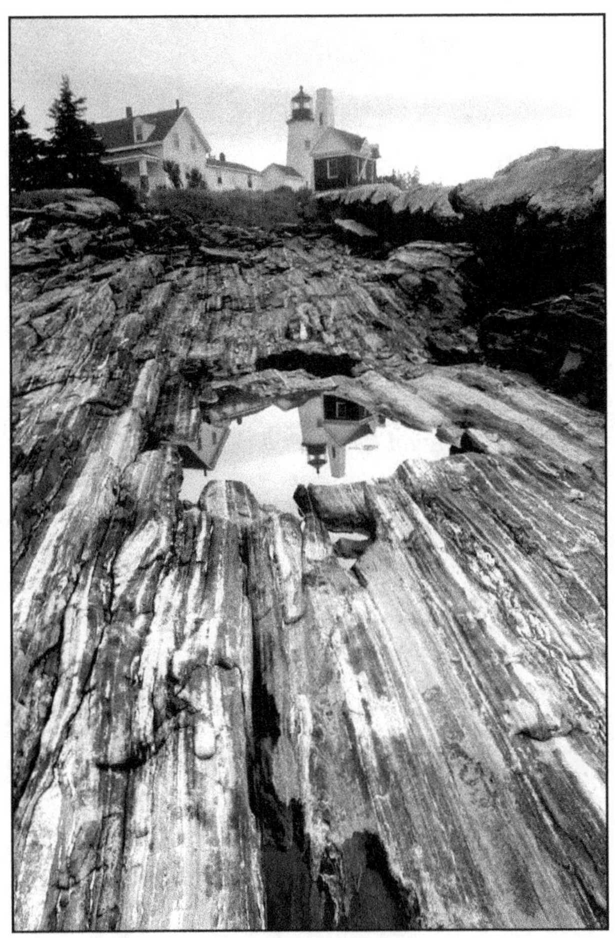

All photos of iconic travel destinations such as this one of Pemaquid Point, Maine, need updating regularly. No matter how many times a place has been photographed, editors always look for new and updated photos.

Historians credit the first photograph to Joseph Nicephore Niepce of France who, in 1826, made an eight-hour exposure on a pewter plate treated with bitumen.

Contents

Joseph Nicephore Niepce combined the camera obscura with photosensitive material in 1826 and then teamed with Louis Daguerre in 1829 to develop the Daguerreotype.

Make And Sell Digital Travel Photos

Introduction

If you want to sell your travel photos to web magazines, print magazines, or place them with stock agencies for sale to web magazines, print magazines, and textbooks, the digital camera and computer have made that job a whole lot easier than it ever was.

This book will help you get your photos published by dividing the process into two parts. The first part is about making travel photos that have a value in the editorial market, travel photos that you can sell. The second part covers the techniques used in finding and approaching the editors who will buy the rights to use your photos.

It is one thing for you to make technically sound and artistically pleasing photos, but to make photos that have marketable value and then to know how to present them to buyers is quite another. This book will get you started on the fast track to selling the rights to your travel photos.

What Has Changed?

Digital imaging is changing rapidly. In fact in this book I have updated the 2008 and 2010 versions in an attempt to keep the info timely.

Changing nearly annually is the digital camera as it upgrades in speed and megapixels. These changes in the digital camera have made it possible for beginning photographers to rapidly develop their skills and to make photos of marketable quality. At the same time the computer, the digital printer, and the fast upload speeds of the web have made it much easier for photographers to reach the photo editors with quality samples of their work.

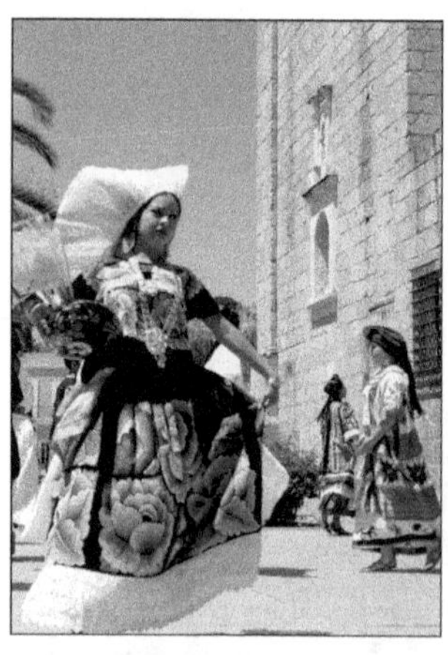

Your iconic photos express the essence of a place and will have value as part of a travel article or a photo feature.

Digital Camera

The digital camera is great for proofing while on location. It offers a powerful tool for improving our image making with its ability to make an almost unlimited number of photos without added expense. The digital camera also becomes a great tool for teaching us to edit as it forces us to be discriminating and to cull out the bad stuff or run out of space on our hard drives.

While the digital camera might have increased our workload by making us the processor, the printer, and the archivist, it has brought us more control than ever over our image making.

Computer

The computer and digital printer allow you to make digital prints of sample photos inexpensively for an editor's review. With your computer you create professional presentations, either as digital files or as files to be printed. These samples are sent in letters, clean and professionally labeled, that will tempt an editor to give you their time and a fair look at your photos.

Digital Freedom

Digital imaging has freed you to get your photos published with less need for technical expertise. New imaging software encompasses a complete set of tools that were formerly only available in the chemical darkroom. These tools give you precise control of your images and the ability to improve them post-production.

After you master a few of the basic imaging tools, you can make digital and printed samples of your work and then email or post the samples with little expense to a photo editor for review.

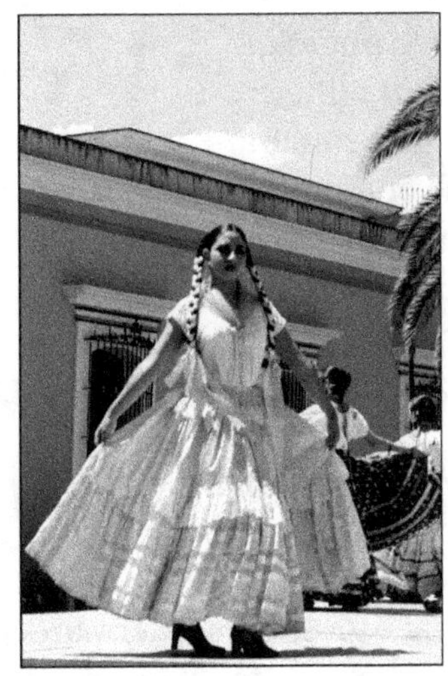

Digital Copies

Once you receive an assignment, the computer has made it less expensive for you to deliver your photos. You do not mail out original slides, negatives, or prints; you make digital copies of your digital photos and you send them via the internet.

You will send them over a phone line, cable modem, FTP site, or as an email attachment. You are now free of postage costs, insurance costs, tracking fees, lost images, scratches on your slides, and a host of other expenses that might have stopped you in the past.

You don't even concern yourself with the return of the material; you have digital copies.

The computer then helps you to track submissions, and helps you to make copies of images for repeat sales in non-competing markets with the same photos.

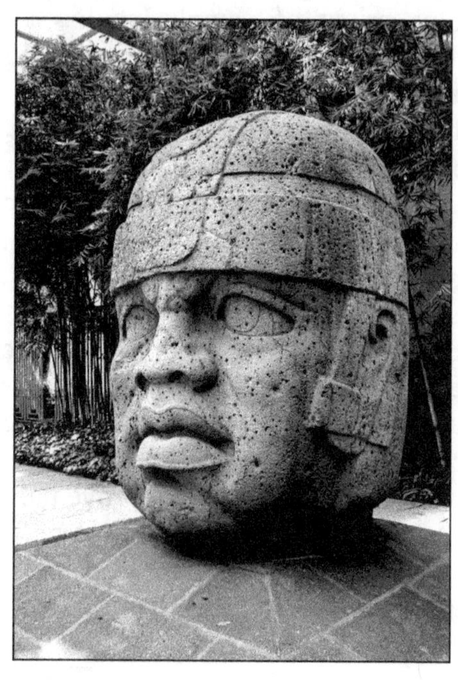

Photos of archaeological artifacts and ruin sites such this Olmec Culture head in the Jalapa Museum, Veracruz, Mexico are often purchased by textbook publishers through a stock photo agency.

In all, the digital camera, the computer, and the web have made the entire process accessible to any beginning photographer.

You Are Invited

Although the popularity of digital imaging and the web has decreased the number of print magazines that buy rights to photos, there are still thousands of print editors and web editors who invite the beginning photographer to be a part of it all. The digital tools have made it easier than ever for you to get your photos out there for review. At this moment there is a new web magazine, print magazine, industry newspaper, or stock agency emerging with a new editor hunting for a unique take on the travel world and that editor is ready to review the digital images that express your special slant on the travel experience.

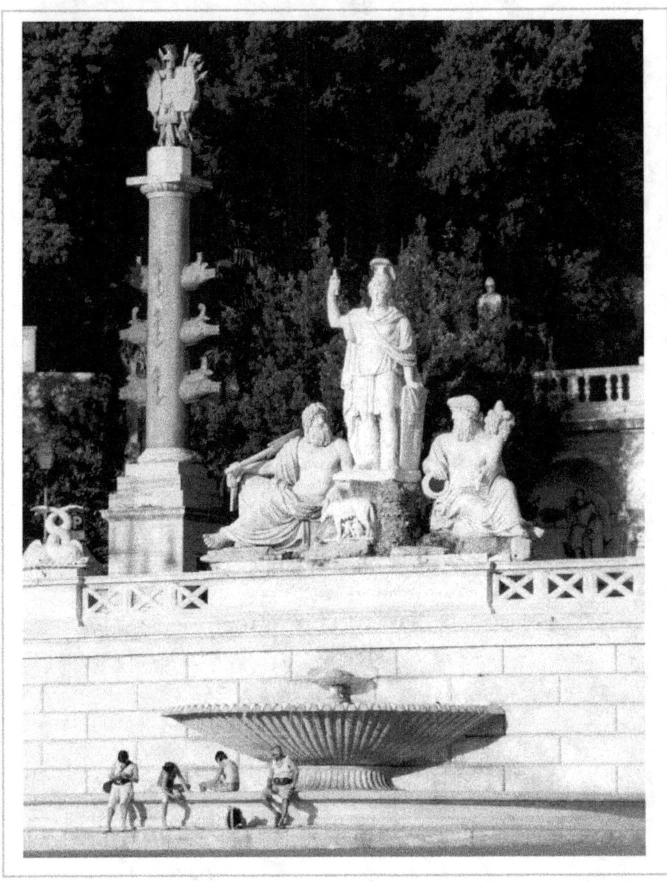

In this Rome street scene, travel photographer Rain Rodolph found a good iconic subject in this fountain; she then waited for some people to enter the scene to give the image added interest and scale.

Photos of events and places such as festivals in Provence, ruins in Mexico, or fountains in Rome can tell a story about the place in an instant.

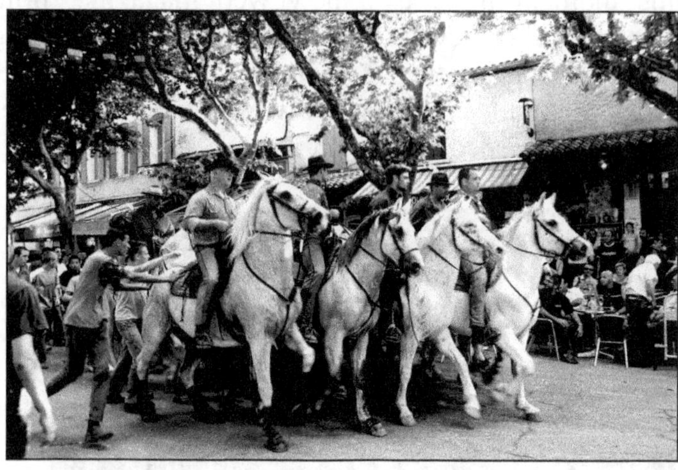

If your photos can express the essence of a place they will have value as part of a travel article, as a photo feature, or as a stock photo with an agency.
In this image the photographer pre-set the focus and the exposure in manual mode while waiting for the horses to fill the scene

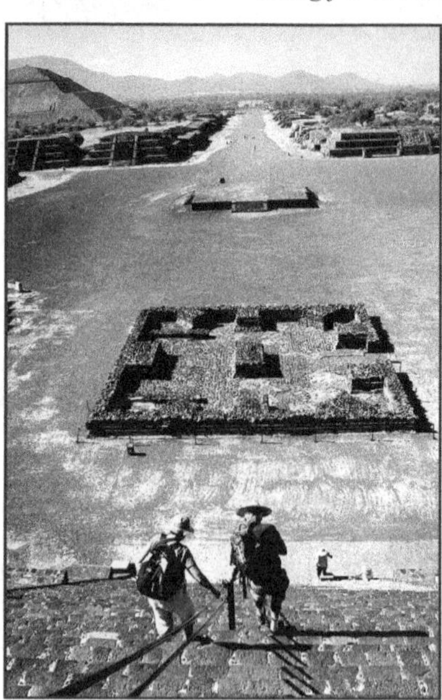

Here the photographer set up the shot, prepared the camera's focus and exposure, and then waited for friends to descend the steps and give scale and the feeling of accessibility to the ruin site.

In 1839, the French Government purchased the rights to the process developed and improved by Niepce and Daguerre and made the technique known to the public.

Make And Sell Digital Travel Photos

Part One

Create Photos That Will Sell

Chapter One, Photos That Will Sell

You do not need to be a great photographer to make and sell travel photos but you do need to know what type of photos will sell. A thorough study of travel websites, web travel magazines, stock agency samples on the web, or print travel magazines will reveal the essence of a marketable photo.

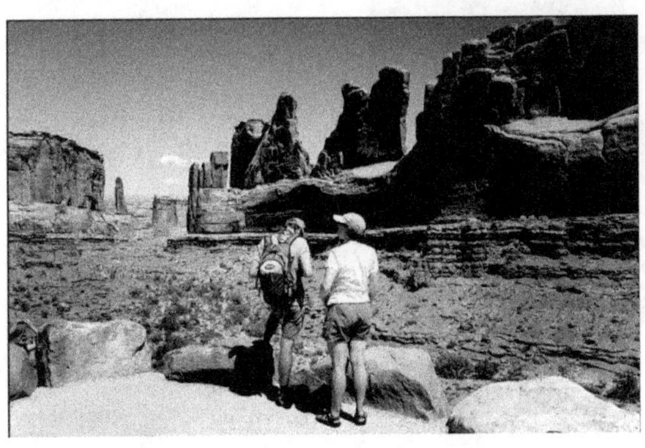

In this photo of Arches NP in Moab, Utah, the photographer found the good background and then backed up to include fellow hikers.

In most published travel photos you will find a good background, well-balanced lighting, and average people enjoying a travel activity.

The travel photo creates a sense of the place and the feeling that you the reader can go to the place and enjoy it just like the people in the photo are doing. The photo creates a feeling of accessibility, freedom, wide-open space, escape, recreation, shopping, romance, and fun.

Marketable Photos

You can make marketable photos like the ones you see on line and in magazines while on your vacation if you find a scenic background with good natural light and then photograph your friends or family hiking, snorkeling, horseback riding, shopping or a dozen other travel activities.

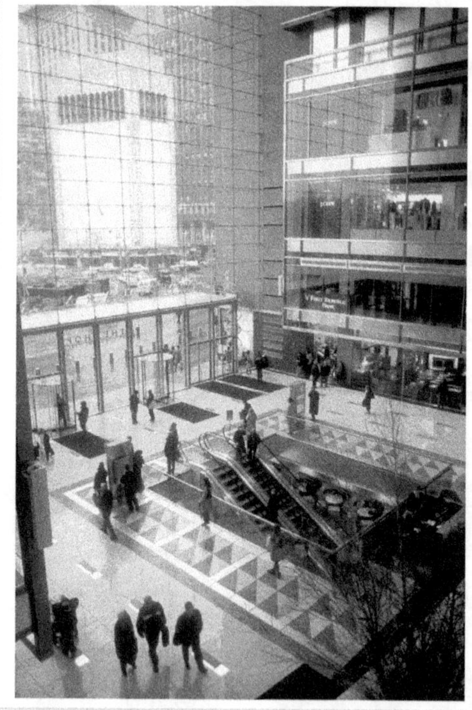

Make photos from up high and down low. Vary your viewpoint to make your photos different.

Set aside some time during your vacation to make several of these photos involving your family and companions as models. Have your friends and family just act naturally, preferably not looking at the camera, not posing. Set up the tripod or use a handy table or fence to prop the camera, use the camera's timer, and jump in the scene yourself. You will have no problem getting the model release there.

Clothing

Clothing will be an important consideration with your models. If you can avoid logos on clothing, avoid brand name products in the photo, and avoid advertising billboards or signs in the background, you can create marketable photos while on vacation. Photos free of logos are vacation photos that could sell.

Set aside some time to make marketable travel photos but remember to leave some time for non-photo vacation fun or you might alienate your models and your companions as their faces turn rigid and they balk at having to continually pose.

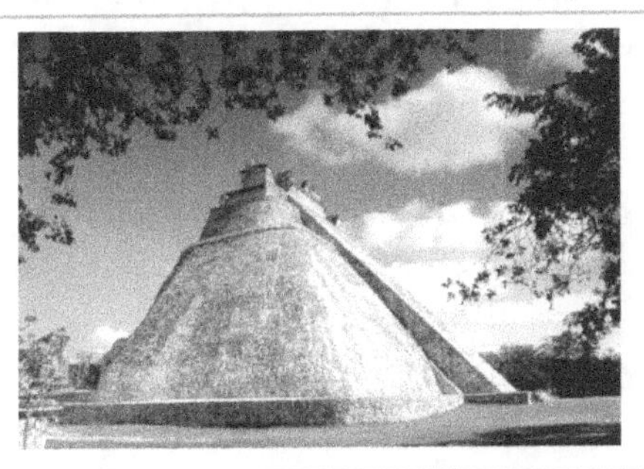

This photo of Uxmal archaeological site gives not much sense of the size of this Mayan building.

Include People In Your Photos

The key is to put people in the scene to give the photo scale and to let the reader know that the place is accessible and that they can go there just as you did

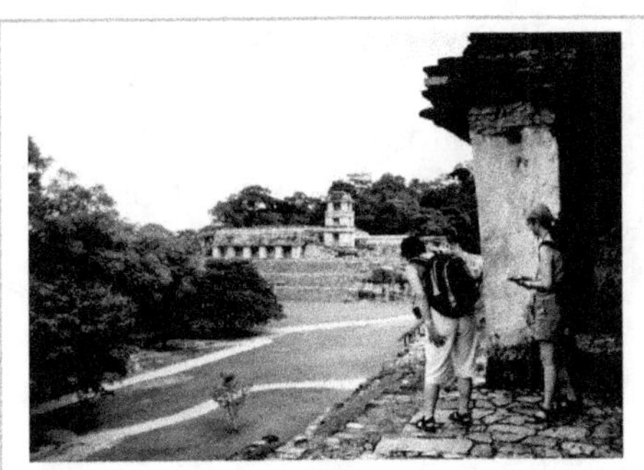

In this photo of the Mayan archaeological site, Palenque in Chiapas, Mexico, people give the photo of buildings scale and show that they are accessible

Model Release

When posing models, including your friends and family, it is a valuable practice to ask permission in the form of a model release (written permission) when the people in the photos are recognizable. This will give the photos more value in a wider market. (See sample Model Release, written permission to use the photos, in chapter seven)

Photo editors prefer average people in the scene, not the professional model; they want the guy or gal next door to which the readers can feel a kinship.

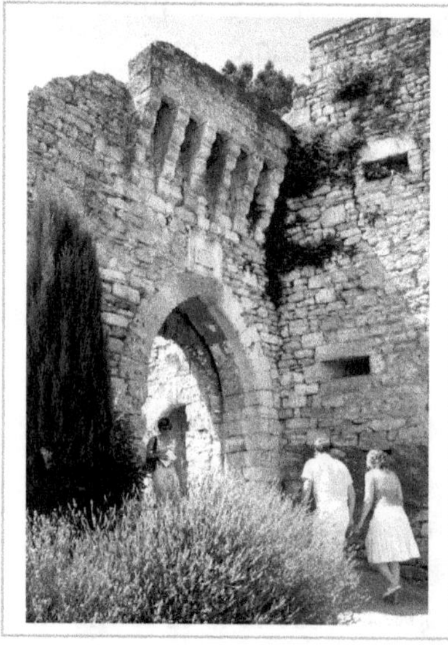

This photo in the Village of Lacoste, Provence, would have had more value as a potential cover if the photographer had left some space at the bottom for cover text and a mailing label

The editors of travel magazines, on occasion, want a model release although, for editorial content such as a travel article, they don't legally need a release.

If you intend to place the photo with a stock photo agency, however, you will in most cases need a release of recognizable people in the photo.

It is best to get a release whenever possible because the release will give the photo more value in diverse markets.

Covers

It is good practice to make both horizontal and vertical photos.

A print magazine editor could use one of your photos as a cover photo if you have made some vertical photos.

A magazine cover or travel brochure cover can bring you $300 and up but will usually be a vertical photo. You should, therefore, make an equal number of vertical images, leaving room at the top of the frame and at the bottom of the frame for the magazine logo and other text that the layout artist will drop in. These photos have more potential value to you as covers.

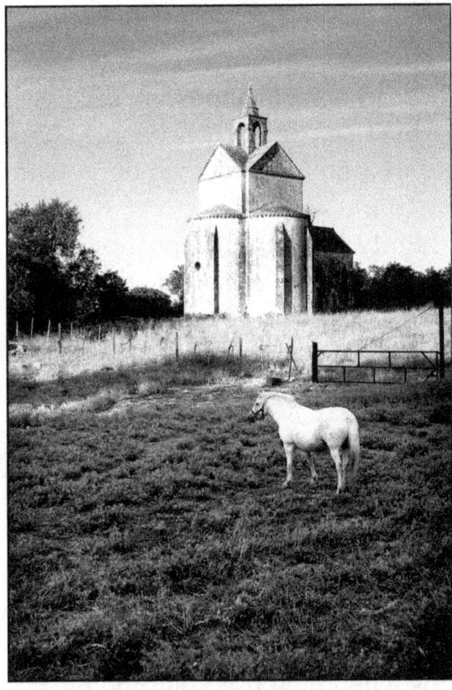

This photo might have better cover potential because the photographer centered the subject and left space for cover text

You will have better chances for sales if your photos offer the editor flexibility and choice when it comes time to lay out the book or magazine pages. If you offer both verticals and horizontals, you will give the photo editor options and a good supply of verticals will give you a chance at a cover.

If your vertical image will withstand enlargement to 8 x12 inches at 300 ppi (Explained in Ch.6) and you have left adequate space at the top for the magazine logo and at the bottom for the mailing label and other text, you will have a good chance at having a more valuable cover photo.

Models

There is the likelihood that your friends and family will not want to pose continually and have their vacation turned into a work assignment. In that case, set up in a place with story-telling background and wait for other people to fill the scene. If the people are not recognizable, you may not need a model release .

You can also ask people to model for you and you will find that quite often people do enjoy the process and do give you the model release if you approach them with kindness and respect. Don't be offended if people refuse, however, there are many reasons why people do not want their photo taken.

If your friends and family get into the spirit of making some photos, pose them enjoying vacation activities in a place where a scenic area will act as a backdrop to tell a more compelling story about the place. Your friends will have fun with it later when they see their photos on the web or in a magazine.

Beige and pastel colored clothing works best, while black or white clothing might loose all detail.

Use appropriate props such as sports equipment, a backpack, or camping equipment for an outdoor theme.

Make sure that the background has no billboards or trademarked items; photo buyers do not want any chance of legal issues with logos when they use your photos.

If possible get signed permission (model release sample, chapter 8) to use the photo; this will give the photo added value, particularly as an image you might place with a stock photo agency.

Clip Book

Before you leave for vacation, make a clip book of photos cut from your favorite travel magazine to use as a guide in posing your models. Use your creativity to build upon the poses and situations that you have seen in travel magazines. These are photos that have sold and will sell again. Make photos like them and you will sell and no, you do not need the latest and greatest camera, but you will want to have a camera that makes the job easier for you.

More about the technical aspects of the equipment that you will need in Chapter 3.

People

Editors will tell you in their photographer's guidelines that they want people in the photos, often requesting that 95 % of your photos have people in them.

When There are No People

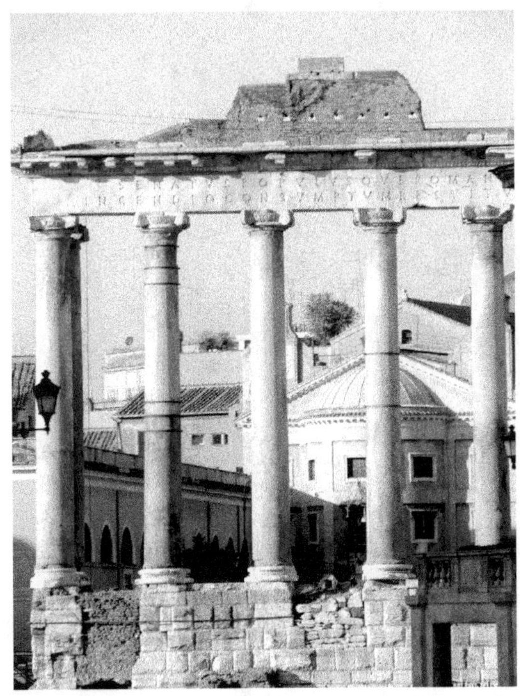

Rome, Rain Rodolph Photo

You can often include the things that people use or places where people once lived, such as ruin sites, to stand in for people while making photos on vacation and still give a sense of the place and a sense of the vacation experience.

Photos That Sell

When you visit the city center look for ethnic festivals where people in regional dress and people participating in ethnic customs will make an interesting photo. Make photos of people in costume, photos of people enjoying exotic foods, and people participating in ethnic folk dance.

If you find an interesting ethnic dance group, for example, back up a little when making some of the photos and include the people watching. These are tourists, the people who will read your web article or magazine spread.

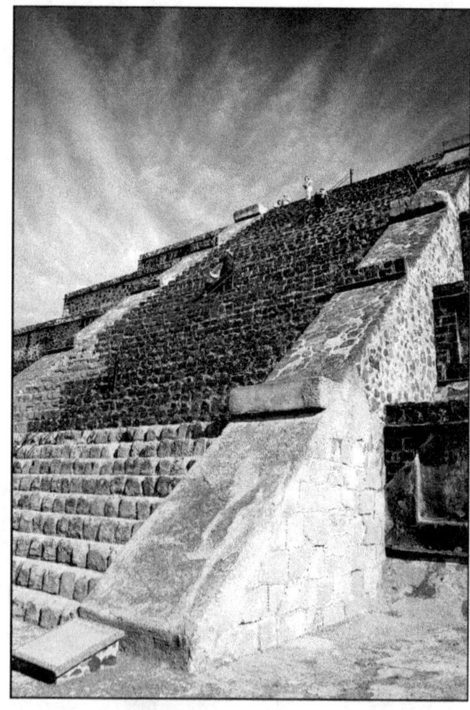

In places such as this, the Teotihuacan archaeological site in Mexico, wait for people to fill the scene to give the photo a sense of scale, added interest, and sense of accessibility

People And Privacy

When photographing people in their villages and in exotic destinations, try to consider their right to privacy while at the same time making photos that tell their story.

Easier said than done you might say. Here are a few thoughts.

Image yourself out in your front yard mowing the lawn one Saturday morning dressed in your worst pair of shorts and a ripped tee shirt. A stranger comes driving down your street and suddenly stops his car. He and his wife jump out and, without hesitation, they point cameras at you. They take your picture, snapping away like crazy. They then jump back in the car and roar off without even a smile, a wave, or a nod of the head. In fact they did not even acknowledging that you exist.

Are you offended? Should they have at least asked permission? Should they have at least thanked you?

Think about this next time you are photographing in a country foreign to you. People around the world are not much different then you; they like their privacy in their front yards and on their streets and they like it when you show respect.

Ask permission before making a photograph and you will be surprised at how often people smile and say yes.

Sometimes they get into the spirit of it. At times they even invite you into their home; they like the fact that you respected them enough to ask.

Sure you will get some that say no; but there are many reasons why people say no and you should not take it as a personal affront. Often people just don't like the way they look. They don't usually dress in shorts and a tattered tee shirt perhaps.

One nice door opener, if you will be in one place for a week or more, is to bring back a photo of the person who posed for you.

It is well worth your time to learn to say, "May I take your photo?" in the language of the country that you plan to visit.

Use this expression whenever you want to make a photo of a stranger and you will be surprised how the interchange becomes rewarding for both parties.

Taking photos of strangers is not without pitfalls, however. People often want you to send them a print and this can get expensive and time consuming.

There could be a blessing here, however. When people ask for a print or you offer a print, you have a great opportunity to get the model release if you have made a photo that you believe will be viable with a stock agency.

Another good way to get in-depth coverage of an area is to do volunteer work. You could use your camera to help a local artisan with a website in exchange for photos of their carving, or weaving process.

If you have made contact with a family, offer to make a family portrait. Offer a shop keeper advertising photos. There are many ways to make deeper coverage in a country that you are visiting.

Most often, however, you will take photos of friends and family on vacation. Photos of people on vacation and people enjoying a new and interesting place resonate with readers of web travel sites and travel magazines. They want to imagine that they can do just what you did and go to an exotic place or interesting city and make photos like you made. Your photos make a trip a reality for the reader and present a place that is reachable and full of promise.

In the next chapter we look at the work of the digital freelance photographer and how the photographer creates those photos full of promise.

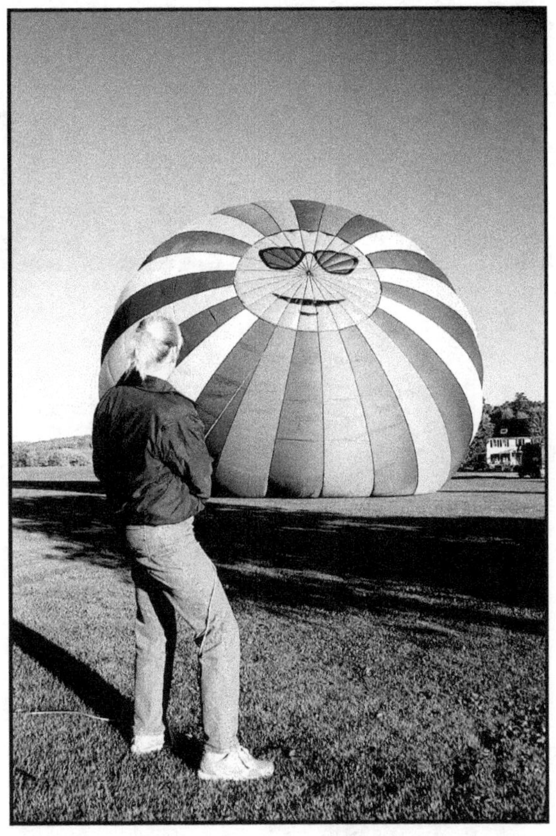

Include people in your photos. Editors of web travel magazines and print magazines want 95% of the photos they use to have people in them.

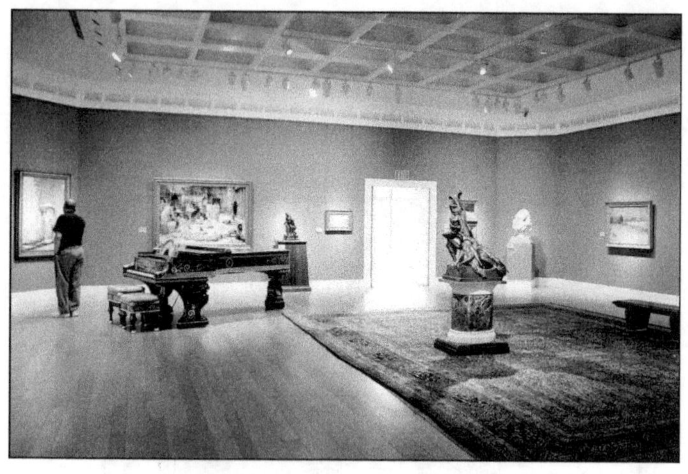

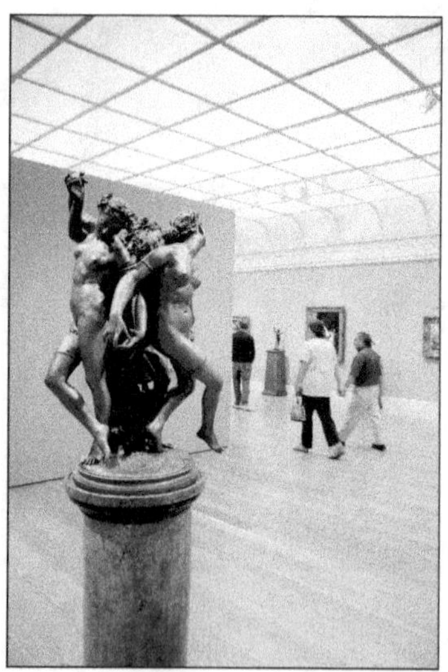

Make both vertical and horizontal photos to give the photo editor options in laying out a web page, brochure, or travel magazine article.

While Daguerre was improving the technique developed by he and Niepce, Englishman William Henry Fox Talbot was creating a process of making negatives on paper bathed in silver chloride and salts, described in 1834 and introduced by him in a book of photographs printed in 1844.

Chapter Two, The Freelance Digital Photographer

Digital photography has opened up a world of markets for the aspiring photographer. The photographer wishing to sell, however, must first decide on a target market.

The beginning freelance digital photographer has three ready avenues open for sales of rights to publish their work: a photo feature in a web magazine, trade journal, or print magazine, a full feature with text and photos in a magazine or trade journal, and photo sales through a stock photo agency. The process of placing images with each of these markets is similar and will be covered in depth in subsequent chapters of this book.

In publishing today the photographer must deliver a digital product. If you are making images with a digital camera you are heading in the right direction. If you prefer to use film or want to use your archived film, slides, or prints, you are still very much in the game but you will need a 4,000 dpi scanner to prepare your images for delivery to the photo editors who buy publishing rights to the work of freelancers.

With the 4000 dpi scanner you scan slides or negatives and deliver high-resolution image files to the web magazines, print magazines, and web portal stock agencies that are good targets for your travel images.

Although a few magazines and stock agencies still accept, and at times prefer, medium and large format transparencies, the beginning freelancer will most often deliver a photo as a digital file made with a 35mm camera. You therefore need to learn how to create and deliver a digital product.

Small Format

Digital imaging with a 35 mm camera is the preferred mode for the small format freelancer, those that supply the web travel magazines, newspapers, and trade papers that have less stringent production demands than the glossy publications that accept only large-format files and transparencies. The field opened wide for the photographer using small-format digital equipment when 35 mm digital cameras approached the 8-megapixel range.

Eight Megapixels

Although publications have long used digital images of a small file size, a digital image from an 8 megapixel camera will come close to matching the quality, sharpness, and lack of grain that low-speed (100 ISO) film produces when taken with a 35 mm camera.

With the digital camera you do not need the added expense of scanning your images, nor does the editor; they go from your camera to your computer and then directly to the editor as a jpeg via phone line, cable modem, or even jump drive, remote hard drive, or flash card.

Many photographers still use their film cameras for more critical work delivered to the high-end, glossy magazines and for their medium and large-format stock photography, scanning the images or sending them for a scan by the editor or agency. As digital cameras have improved, however, and are now in the 18-40+ megapixel range, fewer editors are accepting film; they can cut out the scanning expense if you send quality digital files

Changes

Digital equipment has rapidly changed the industry. Not long ago, magazines would accept prints or negatives that they would then photograph for the making of plates for inking in the four-color printing process. This process used cyan, yellow, magenta, and black. Each color would have its photographic separation for the making of plates and the print house would ink these etched plates for the final print.

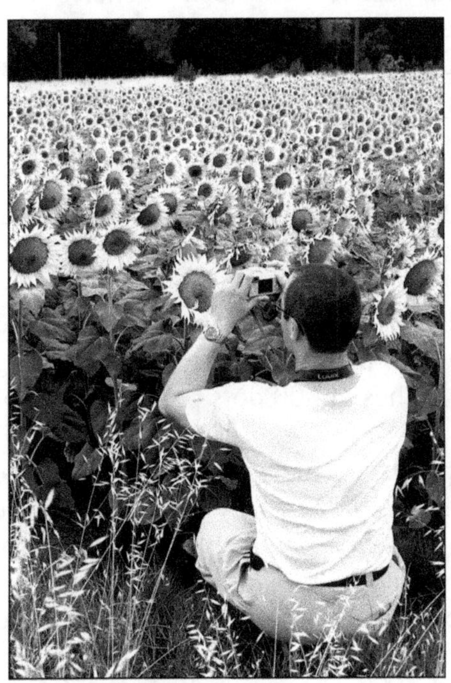

Sunflowers in Provence, France

Digital equipment has changed the process and continues to revolutionize the printing industry.

With the introduction of

digital printing equipment, a color slide, transparency, negative or scanned print would go to the editor's computer and then to the print house for the separation done digitally, bypassing the intermediate use of film for the making of separate color plates.

Now, more often than not, the editor will request digital TIFF (Tagged Image File Format) images burned to a CD or they will want Jpeg (Joint Photographic Experts Group) images sent over a phone line to the editor's computer.

Some editors will request raw files sent via CD. (Raw explained Ch. 6) The editor will eliminate the scanning and the generation of film separations as the computer performs the separation of colors and feeds the layout of the images and text directly to the printer for the laser burning of thin plastic or aluminum printing plates.

Photo editors at magazines and stock agencies will most often request that you send them a digital file. If you can deliver a clean, unsharpened digital file, sized to the editors request, you are well into the game.

Web Sales

Many photo buyers shop for images through a stock agency on the web and they receive delivery over a DSL (Digital Subscriber Line) phone line. If you decide to work with an agency, a typical stock agency photo editor’s request might be that you send an 8-bit jpeg image, sized to 8 x 12 inches at 300 dots per inch (dpi) or Pixels per inch (ppi).

Dots per inch and pixels per inch are terms that people often use interchangeably although they do not mean the same thing. You can, however, use these terms similarly in correspondence with editors. *(Explained In Glossary)*

You could be asked to burn these files to a CD and then send them through the mail but more than likely you will be asked to send them as 8 x 12 inch, 300 dpi Jpeg files sent over a computer modem phone line. Requests vary greatly.

Scanning of Slides, Prints, and Negatives

The three avenues to sales mentioned earlier, the web or print magazine photo feature, the feature article, and the stock agency, work in a similar fashion.

You first make a proposal and once you receive an acceptance or an assignment, you supply photo files.

If you are making images with film or using archived film or prints you will need to scan your negatives, slides, or prints for the creation of digital files and the creation of inkjet-printed samples.

Epson, Microtek, and others make low-cost scanners that will scan slides, negatives, and prints at high optical resolution, above 4000 dpi. A Scanner with an optical resolution of 4000 or above will be more than adequate for publishable files of negatives or slides in web magazines, print magazines, and newspapers. These scanners will cost less than $200.

Image Size

When you create these images in your imaging software you will have unlimited size options. Once you make a sale, however, you must create the files as the editor requests. You could get many and varied requests for file sizes so you should begin learning how to use imaging software to size your images for delivery. That will be crucial to your participation in this process; you must learn to size and deliver images to an editor's exact request and you must stay up to date with the editor's needs as those needs change. (More on sizing in Chapter 10)

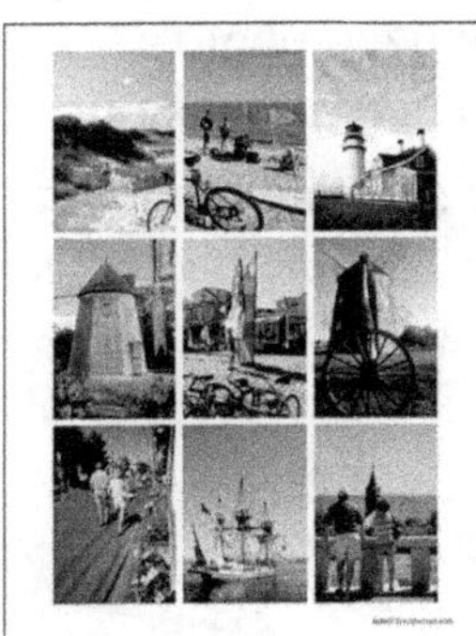

Samples

During the preparation of a proposal, you will make digital color files of samples sent as jpeg attachments or color prints that you will then send as samples along with a business letter to an editor for review.

Your color printer will allow you to create inexpensive sample pages of photos. You might need many low-cost digitally printed samples of your work when starting out. You will more than likely approach several or perhaps many editors and agencies with letters and samples.

Although a few magazine photo editors and stock agencies still review duplicate slides or prints, the shipping expense to deliver and return the material and to insure it is prohibitive. A better option is to make a high-resolution scan and a 300 dpi inkjet print containing samples of your work for a photo editor's review. You can do this with much less expense. (*More about Sample photos in Chapter Nine*)

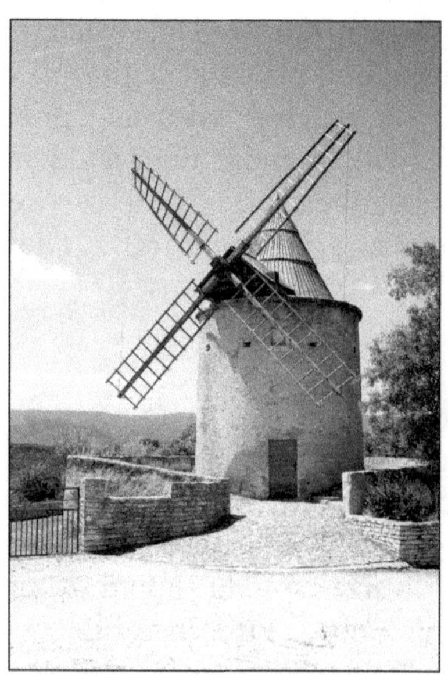

For a travel photo feature about a place, the iconic building like this Provence windmill would be a key part of a submission of photos.

Once you reach your travel destination, you will need some slightly specialized photo equipment to make the job of creating photos easier. The next chapter looks at tools that will help the traveling digital photographer make marketable travel photos.

In 1841, Talbot patented his process called the Calotype. Improvements made by others, notably the albumen process, made the making of photographic plates easier. Photography still required long exposures and photographers could only use it for architecture or landscapes.

Chapter Three, Tools Of The Traveling Photographer

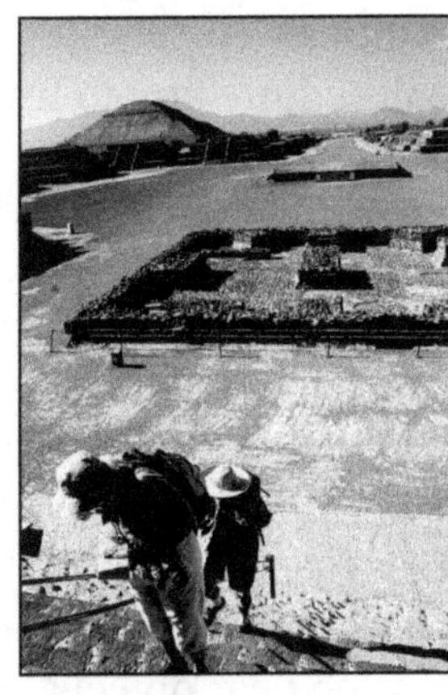

Manually set the focus to include a sharp background, mid ground and foreground. In this photo the movement of the people in the foreground might have shifted the focus to blur the background

When you make marketable photos with your digital camera to you must be able to manage a few details. In this chapter we look at features that a digital camera should offer to make the job easier.

Ideal Camera

The ideal digital camera would allow you the option of working in manual mode. In fact manual mode will be indispensable if you are to create a wide variety of marketable photos.

Manual Control

We love our automatic gadgets but you can be more creative if you take control of your camera.

If you can control your camera's aperture, shutter speed, and focus in manual control mode, you will have a versatile camera that will work well in the rapidly changing situations that you will encounter while making travel photos for publication.

You will run into many situations, especially when using fill flash, where you need to override the automatic camera functions and work in manual mode. This is particularly true when you combine ambient light and flash photography; you need to have control of your shutter speed and the aperture.

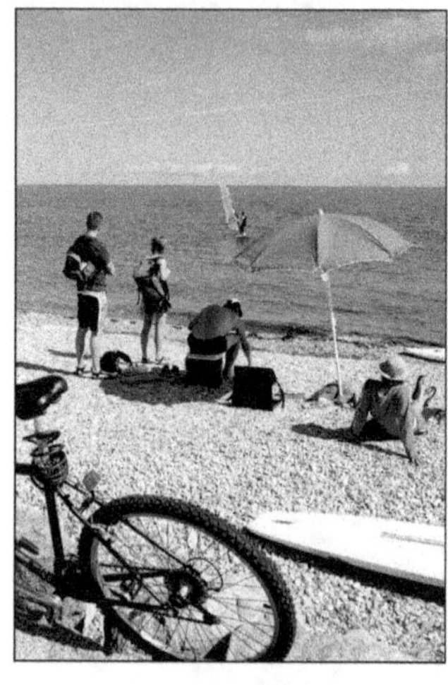

Manual focus will allow you to photograph near ground, mid ground, and background sharply and shoot continually regardless of any moving subjects

You will also run into the problem of lenses that focus automatically in well-lit areas but have trouble focusing in darker situations. This problem will require you to use manual focus.

Lens Hunting

Another problem with automatic focusing lenses comes with moving targets or with people crossing in front of you while you make photos. The auto focus will hunt rapidly between near objects and distant objects

Flash Cord Port

Another good feature to have on a camera is a port that allows you to plug in a cord for the running of a remote flash when you want lighting more interesting than that provided by the built-in, on-camera flash unit.

Battery Life

You will want to get a day or more of making photographs from one battery and have a backup ready to go.

Preview Window

A well-sized preview window will help you in proofing your images while on the move.

Megapixels

There is much discussion about how many megapixels a camera should have to make photos for publication. Most photographers agree that at eight megapixels, the digital camera approaches the film camera as a standard for the making of printable or publishable images in a glossy magazine.

This does not mean that you cannot make marketable images with a four or five megapixel camera. Images made with three and four megapixel cameras have been printed in magazines and newspapers for years. To give yourself a chance at stock sales, travel, trade, and perhaps fine art calendar markets, however, the more megapixels the better.

For the freelancer just starting out, the moderately priced camera will come in at between ten and 15 megapixels.

Several stock agencies request that you use nothing smaller than a 10-megapixel camera.

Minimum File Size

The usual minimum for a newspaper or a magazine will be an 8 x 10 inch, jpeg or TIFF image at 300 dpi. This results in a file size of about 24 megabytes. If your camera can make a file that will result in a TIFF this size after conversion and possible minor interpolation, you can deliver high quality images to an editor.

Although a newspaper photo editor might be happy with an 8 x10 jpeg at 300 ppi, for you to supply photos for high-paying covers in glossy magazines or to have your photos represented by a stock agency, you will need to offer TIFF files as large as 13x19" at 300 ppi. This file could be approximately 60 megabytes in size.

You will be far better equipped to offer photos to diverse markets if you use an 10-megapixel or higher camera.

Single Lens Reflex Camera

A good option that would include all these features and more would be a single lens reflex camera. (DSLR) The DSLR will provide the features mentioned and will also allow you to attach lens filters and a lens hood to the front of your lenses, important additions that will be described later.

The DSLR will also have a through-the-lens viewing system that will give you precise control of your composition.

Ten Second Timer

Most digital single lens reflex cameras have a ten-second timer as standard equipment. The timer will help you create low-light scenes and interiors in churches, restaurants, and museums with hands-off sharpness after you prop or support the camera.

The SLR will offer features that will make a camera a flexible tool for making travel photos. That is not to say that a range finder or point and shoot couldn't make marketable photos. In fact there are mirror-less cameras that are light and versatile when outfitted with high quality zoom lenses that are producing publishable photos every day. It is just that features of a DSLR such as screw-on lens filters, remote flash ability, and through the lens viewing will make the job of creating publishable travel photos more predictable.

Digital Capture Speed

Digital capture speed is critical when you make photos for publication. You want a camera that allows you to use a low-speed ISO of 100-200 except in special situations of dramatic editorial content.

With a setting in this range, you will avoid the blotchy look called noise that afflicts digital photos taken at high-speed capture or in low light. Noise in high ISO digital capture and grain in high-speed film can ruin an otherwise marketable photo. This will apply to film but will vary a great deal in the different camera brands. Follow the photographers guides.

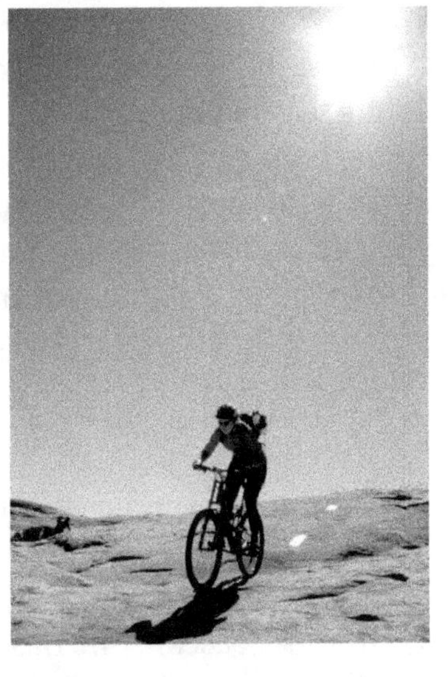

Obvious lens flare, and in this case intentional to show a hot day.

The damaging flare is one that you might not see but it reduces contrast. You can avoid it by the use of a lens shade or lens hood.

Lenses

Many digital cameras come equipped with lenses that zoom from 17 mm to 85 mm or higher. If you use a zoom lens that covers this range, you will have adequate lens variety to start out.

The lens set at 17 mm to 35 mm will be important for your photos of people in a setting for sense-of-place images. The 50 mm lens setting will do for landscapes. Your most important photos will be of people in a good background, however, and you will most often do this in the 17-50 mm range.

Lens Shade

The lens should allow you to affix a lens shade. This attachment will be crucial to preventing lens flare and reduction of contrast as it shields the front lens element from the sun and stray light.

Lens flare is not just the obvious blotch in the upper reaches of the frame, such as in the photo on the previous page, but a nearly imperceptible lowering of contrast and saturation that robs a photo of punch and kills an otherwise marketable photo.

Scattered light enters the lens and bounces around and then reaches the sensor or film plane where it brightens up the dark areas, thus reducing the contrast. This can be subtle and nearly imperceptible except that you might find yourself saying that the photo looks washed out.

If your camera does not come equipped to accept a lens shade you can use your hand to protect the lens element from direct sun. If you are using a tripod, step forward and look at the front lens element; if the sun or reflected light is hitting it in any way you are apt to have lens flare.

Balanced Exposure

One of the hallmarks of a marketable photo is an evenly exposed frame. Large areas of the frame in shadow or areas of overexposure where you have blown out detail will not be acceptable in most cases. Fill flash and the graduated neutral density filter will aid in making evenly exposed images.

Fill Flash

One of your important tools is fill flash provided by your on-camera flash or by a remote flash. Good technique with fill flash will elevate your photos from the grab shot or snapshot variety to a more professional level of the created photo. The fill flash is used during daylight photography to punch up the colors, to light under wide brimmed hats, to bring sparkle to the eyes, and to help balance the exposure.

Difficult to use, yes, it takes practice to get it right even with automatic through-the-lens systems that sense the light and control the amount of flash hitting the subject or the amount of flash returning to the sensor.

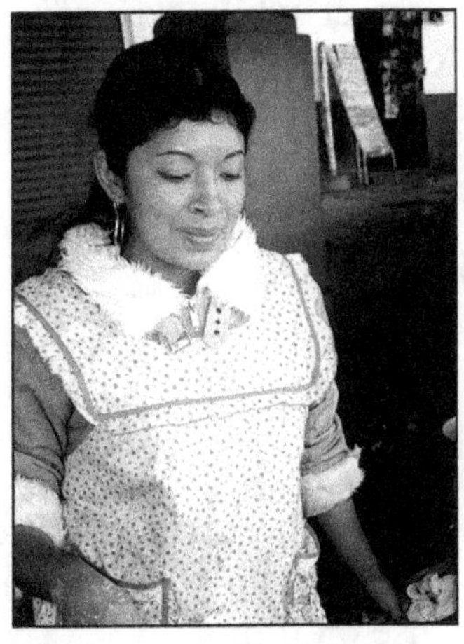

Fill flash, on-camera was used to lighten the right side of the subjects face and balance the exposure.

Diffused Flash

Diffused and bounce flash are best because they are less harsh. It should not be obvious that you used flash.

Practice with known distances and changes of the lens apertures before you go on vacation and you will quickly catch on, particularly if you are using a digital camera and can review your results immediately.

Avoid Redeye

In darkened rooms, redeye can be a problem.

An on-camera flash unit will illuminate the subjects wide-open iris and bounce back to the camera with the red color within the iris showing in your photo. You can avoid this by holding or attaching a remote flash approximately one foot above the lens.

In outdoor photography redeye is usually not a problem.

When you elevate the flash above the lens you also remove the shadow that often falls to one or another side of the subject's face when you use on-camera flash and hold the camera in portrait mode.

You can soften the light if you place a plastic diffuser over the flash unit or, in the tilt head type, tape a bounce card to the back of the flash unit and tilt the head up. If the flash is a harsh, on-camera flash and you have no diffuser handy, a bit of tracing paper or tissue paper over the flash will tone down the brittle light, diffuse it and make it softer.

Practice the use of bounce flash and diffused flash at different distances with a test subject while you adjust aperture and make notes in your clip book.

Filters

If you have a camera with lenses that allow screw-on filters you make available additional tools.

UV Filter

An ultraviolet filter screwed on to the front of the lens is a good tool for protecting your lens.

When film was commonly in use, these filters were needed to absorb the sun's ultra violet light and to prevent a blue cast that UV rays would cause on film.

With digital cameras and with most glass lenses used today, UV is no longer a problem; the optics on most lenses guard against it. The UV filter still has its place, however; it can be a method of protecting your lens from scratches and finger smudges.

When you clean your lens you don't need to clean the actual lens element, which would shorten its life, you clean the less expensive and easily replaced UV filter.

At between $30 and $80 dollars, a UV filter will considerably extend the usable life of your more expensive lenses. Get the best filter that you can afford to preserve sharpness.

Graduated Neutral Density Filter

One of the most important tools for making marketable photos will be a graduated neutral density filter. This will perform the critical balancing of the exposure, often toning down a bright sky and bringing it within a stop of the foreground. You can also tone down a foreground with a graduated neutral density filter when you are using fill flash. (Stops explained further in glossary.)

GND Filter

A two stop graduated neutral density filter (GND) is a good solution to balancing an exposure.

Often there will be a difference of four or even five stops of light between the sky and the foreground when the near ground is in shade on a sunny day. The GND can bring this into better balance.

Use the best filters that you can afford, the quality will be one of the keys to sharpness.

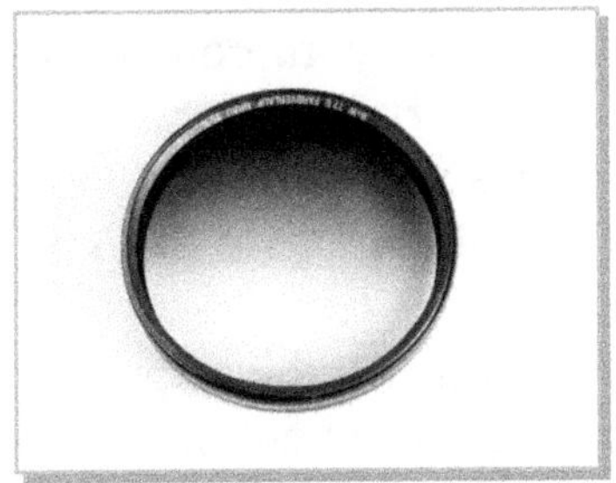

The GND comes in two types; the round glass within a frame that is sized to screw on to the front of the lens, and the rectangular shaped sheet that fits into a holder attached to the front of the lens.

The sheet of GND is the best choice for several reasons; foremost because you can adjusted it in its holder to more accurately tone down an area in the sky or foreground.

GND Positioning

You can rotate the GND left, right, or bottom, depending where the bright area occurs in your frame.

The Cokin brand professional holder, (Cokin P), pictured below is a reasonably priced, screw-on holder that will accept several brands of GND sheet filters for balancing exposure. These 3.25 x 4.65 inch sheets can also be hand-held in front of the lens for quick variety and you can rotate them to tone done any area of the frame, not just the sky.

Price

Graduated Neutral density filters come in varying degrees of quality and price from $40 to $125 dollars. Brands available include Singh Ray, B&W, Hoya, Tiffin, Lee, Cokin, and others.

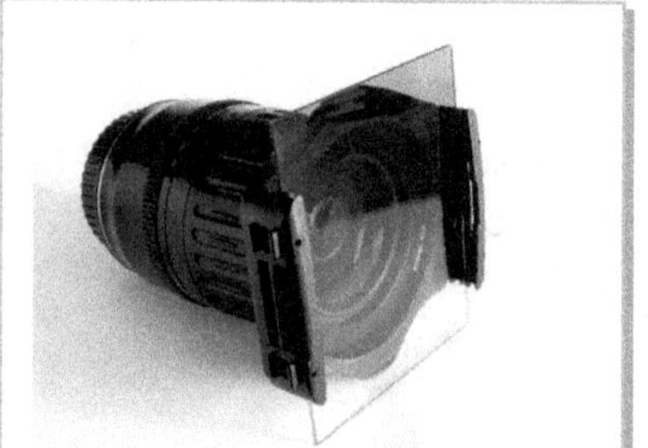

These filters come differentiated by stops: 1-stop, 2-stops, and 3-stops. The manufacturers use two numbering systems: 2x, 4x, 8x, or .03, .06, .09. The 4x or 2-stop is the best compromise if you will use only one filter. If you carry two, get a one-stop and a three-stop because at times you can stack them and compensate for four stops of difference.*(See Photo Equipment Suppliers on reference page, Ch. 10)*

Although you can accomplish considerable exposure balancing in imaging software, it is good time-saving and skills-building practice to make the best photo possible in the camera. Photo editors don't want you to work digital images too severely in the computer. You will find that if you make well-balanced images in the camera it is a whole lot less work and the images are cleaner and free of noise.

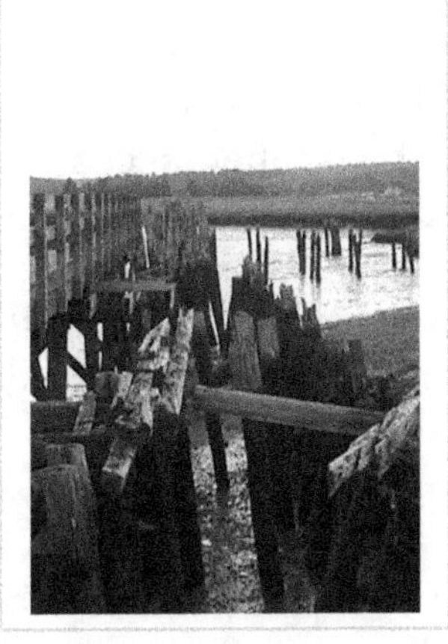

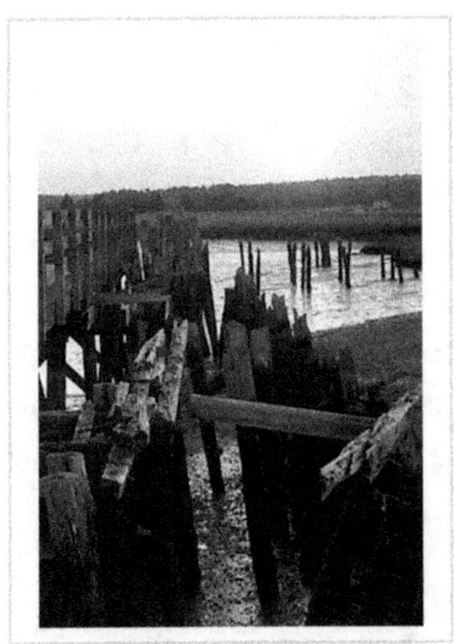

In these two frames, the one on the left had no GND attached to the lens. The sky is completely burned out with no color, just a large area of white with no detail.
With the application of two GND filters totaling four stops, although it does not show in the black and white, the photographer preserved the color detail in the sky.

Practice With Your GND

There is no substitute for in-the-field practice and testing of equipment and techniques. The digital camera has made that all the more affordable and made it so much easier than with film.

The tricky part of working with a GND will be knowing how much balancing of exposure you will need. The quickest way to find out is to use your cameras meter and take readings of the foreground, the mid ground, and the sky without the filter in place.

Usually, on a sunny day, you will find three to four stops of difference. That is to say, the sky might read f-16 at 1/60 of a second and the foreground in shadow may read f-4 at 1/60 of a second. Two clicks of the aperture is one stop if you have set your camera to read in half stops. In this case f-16, f-11, f-8, f-5.6, and f-4.

Once you determine the number of stops between the high and low, you will know how much exposure adjusting to do with your GND or with stacked GNDs.

Take a reading of the lowest light level, usually the foreground in shadow, and set the shutter speed and aperture manually on the camera to match this. They must stay locked.

Then install the GND material. After installing the filter, regardless of what your camera light meter reads, you are ready to make the photo.

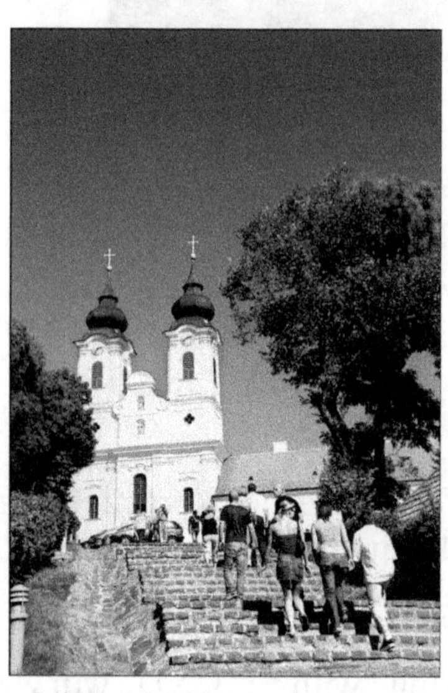

Rain Rodolph Photo

Software Corrections

Computer users will be tempted to do this balancing of exposure in the computer. When you try to balance a difference of four stops in the computer, however, the results are too often disappointing and will not be of publishable quality. Attempts at rehabilitating dark underexposed areas of a frame will result in more work than that required to practice and learn camera techniques that result in publishable photos right from the camera. And remember that photo editors want clean digital files.

Polarizer

The Polarizer or polarizing filter will saturate and accentuate colors, remove reflection, and bring punch to cloudy skies. It becomes an important tool when used at the appropriate time. The polarizer, however, can also turn a cloudless blue sky to black and it will absorb a stop and a half of light, which might make it a problem in hand-held photography on all but the brightest of days when using 100-speed digital capture.

Screw-On Type

The Polarizer usually screws onto the outer ring of the lens and rotates to its most effective position. Regardless of whether it is doing its polarizing work or not, the polarizer still absorbs one and a half stops of light.

The polarizer is most effective if the sun is either 90 degrees to the left or to the right of the photographer and becomes less effective when the sun is to the front or to the rear and less effective also at sunrise and sunset.

Circular or Linear Polarizer

Match the polarizer to the camera type. Most cameras will require a circular polarizer in order for the camera's automatic sensing systems to work properly.

Shutter Speed

You will want complete control of your shutter speed. Your camera should allow you to quickly set the shutter speed while photographing.

Camera Shake

While on the move, you will often be hand-holding the camera while photographing people enjoying travel experiences. You will need to keep in mind the rule of thumb for making photos while hand holding the camera, "match the shutter speed to the focal length of the lens."

Match Shutter Speed To Lens

Unless you have anti-shake lenses (Image Stabilization, IS) or an anti-shake camera body, you will need to be mindful that the movement of your hands can blur the photo unless you have a fast enough shutter speed to freeze the camera motion. The longer the lens (zoom) the more exaggerated this shake becomes.

If you use automatic mode and let the camera determine shutter speed, you will have many blurry photos that show the motion of the camera and the shake of your hands.

With a 60 mm lens, the optimal shutter speed for hand holding the camera and overcoming shake would be 1/60 of a second, a rule of thumb that matches the bottom number of the shutter speed to the lens focal length. Other examples of this rule would be a 1/125 shutter speed to a 125 mm lens and a 1/250 shutter speed when hand holding a 250 mm lens.

This gets tricky with zoom lenses. A good rule of thumb when using zooms is to set the shutter speed for the longest focal length of the zoom lens. This would be 1/250 of a second with a 250 mm zoom lens. Thus set, when you zoom in, you will not need to change to a faster shutter speed to overcome camera shake.

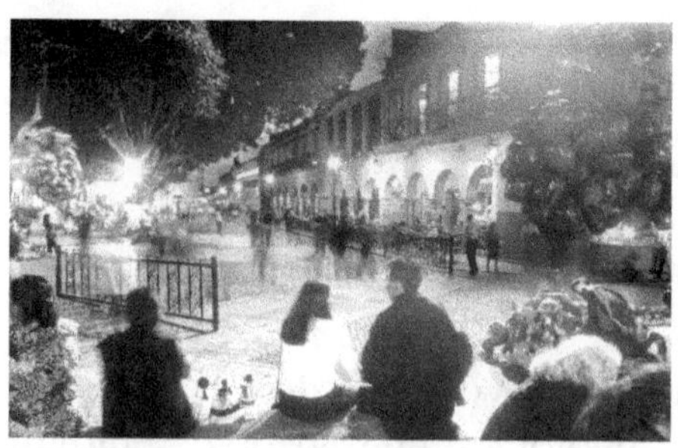

Once you begin mastering the tools of making sharp, well-exposed photos, you can concentrate more on the content of your photos and their value in the market.

Because a high (fast) shutter speed might limit your depth of field sharpness, a good compromise is 1/125 shutter speed while using a zoom lens. Usually you will be trying to capture a moment and not have the presence of mind to change shutter speeds each time you zoom in. This technique will free you from that problem. You will, however, need a camera that has a shutter speed that you can set to manual mode.

Use this rule of thumb and attempt to match the shutter speed to the lens focal length and, as added insurance, steady the camera against a pole, fence, or any handy support. Sharpness is one of the keys to consistently creating marketable photos.

Although you may see great motion blur and un-sharp photos in publication and you should make a few for variety, it is a fashion trend that comes and goes. A portfolio full of un-sharp photos would be a tough sell in the travel photo market.

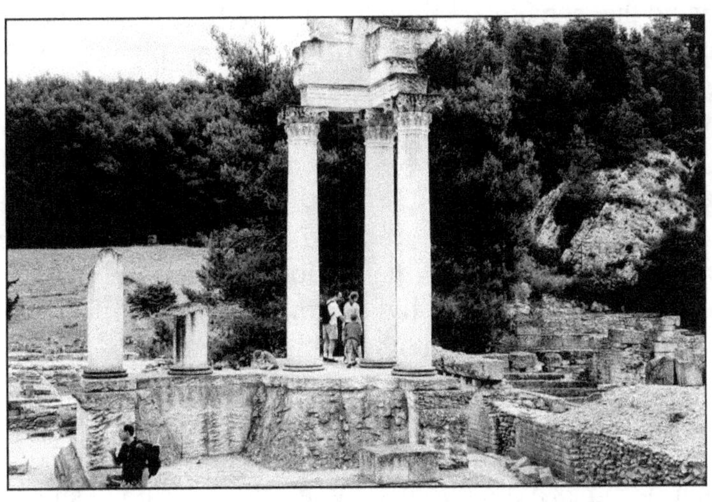

Most of your travel destination photos should be sharply focused and have people in the scene to give the viewer the sense that they too can visit this place.

Tripod

The tripod is a great aid in landscape and low light photography but many museums, churches, and archaeological sites prohibit their use. You should, therefore, practice a few techniques to make interior and low-light photographs without a tripod.

Prop the Camera

In places where authorities prohibit tripods, you can use other techniques to make sharp photos.

Prop the camera on church benches, steady the camera against light poles, and use a beanbag to support the camera on restaurant tables. These techniques will diminish the importance of the tripod.

Place the camera bag on the floor and use the ten-second timer to trip the shutter and you will have a vibration free photo and an unusual point of view.

Although you might develop a dozen techniques to steady the camera, a tripod can still be a great aid to sharpness and an aid in creating complex photos. It is best to bring one on your trip and use it whenever possible.

Bean Bag

Buy a half kilo of beans when you arrive at your destination and have them double bag it loosely. Amaranth seeds make a light beanbag. This will cushion the camera on tables and other handy props.

Ten-Second Timer

There are situations where your camera's ten-second timer becomes a great tool. If you use it to trip the shutter once you prop the camera, you will have hands-off sharpness.

Look into the Joby Gorillapod, a small tripod that fits into the camera bag and has flexible legs that can glom onto church benches, light poles, and many handy supports that will give you a steady shot without shake.

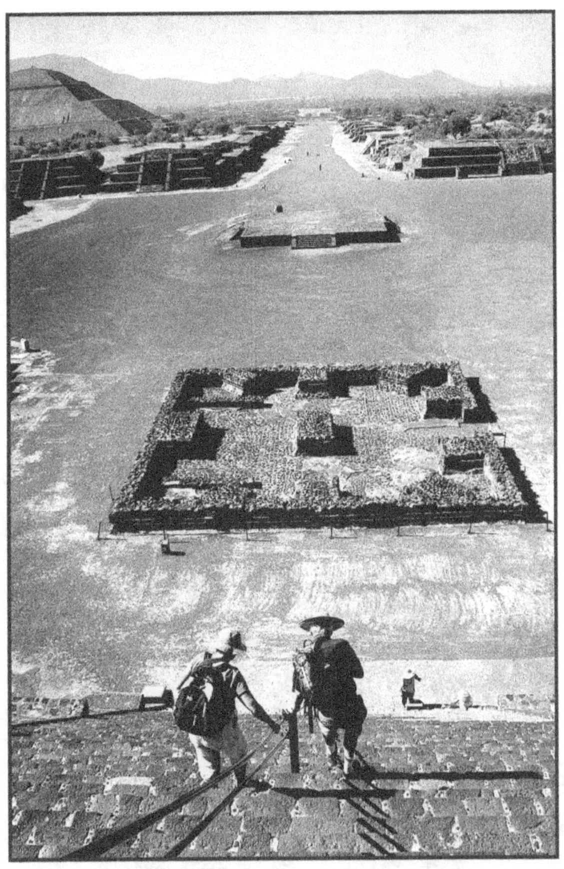

You set up in a place with a good background, pre-focus your camera, use the GND to balance out the exposure, and then have your friends fill the scene.

Put The Tools To Work

More about making marketable photos in the next chapter as we put the tools to work

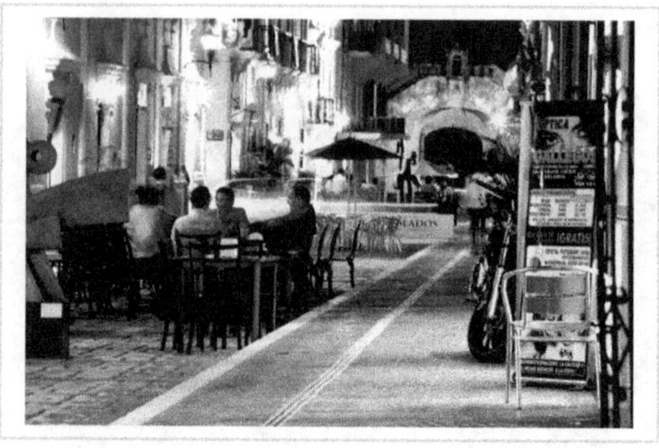

Night photos can be interesting and give a feeling that the vacation place offers nightlife

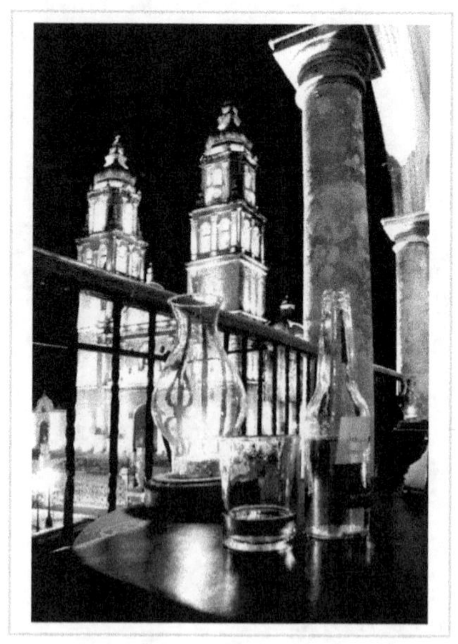

Timothy O'Sullivan, one of the first great travel photographers, made photos in the Grand Canyon in 1872 using the 1851 colloidal wet plate process while he hauled a dark room built in an old horse-drawn first aid wagon.

Chapter Four, Put The Tools To Work

In this chapter we look at the tools, why we have them and how we use them.

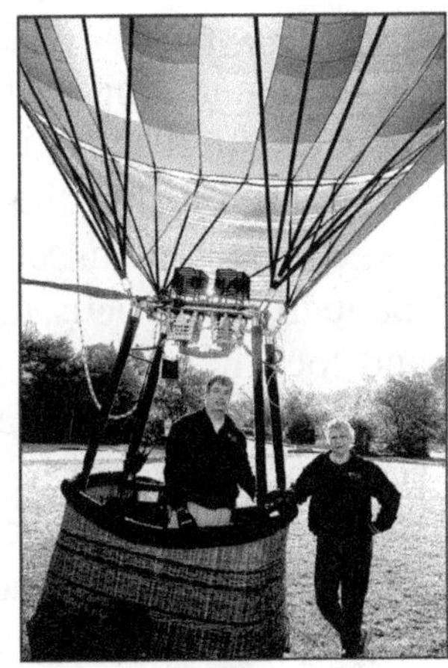

Fill Flash:

Although the subjects in this photo to the right are back-lit, the fill flash illuminated their faces.

In a back-lit scene you must use the camera's manual mode and expose for the subjects, in this case their faces.

Back-lit scenes are interesting but difficult; you can usually improve on the photo by putting the sun at your back and your subject in the light. Just be careful that you don't photograph your own shadow.

Over Expose

One characteristic about digital cameras you will want to keep in mind is that because of the nature of the capture system, you can recover detail in a slightly over exposed section of a frame but will be less successful in correcting an underexposure. When using a digital camera, therefore, you should just slightly over expose rather than underexpose.

Camera Preview Window

One great tool that the digital camera offers is the preview screen. The intensity of this screen is adjustable, however, and it bears mentioning that if you set it too bright, you might be fooled onto thinking your exposures are on the mark when in fact, they will be underexposed. Set your preview intensity to medium at the most.

Photojournalism

Travel photography has evolved through the years to become closer to photojournalism. The landscape, once the signature of travel photography, has become not much more than an important backdrop for photos of people and their vacation activities.

Once you find the good background, you have set the stage. You then set up the tripod or prop the camera, manually pre-focus the lens, manually set your exposure and lock it, and then you fill the scene with your friends and family, or you wait for other vacationers to enter the scene. People tell the story; editors want more than just a striking landscape, they want people in the photos.

With your good background you give the photo a sense of place, when you include people, you add interest, scale, and the message that the place is accessible.

Sense of Place

While making photos in the great backgrounds and places that attract tourists, you hope to create a sense of the place. If you do that you will return from vacation with good coverage for a photo feature. You might even consider a full-length feature travel article about a place where people can go and where they can enjoy the surroundings just as you did.

Creating this sense of people involved in vacation activities like visiting museums and restaurants, shopping, participating in sports, and enjoying beaches, can present you with a host of technical challenges of mixed light and uneven exposure, moving subjects, and clouds that change the exposure by the minute. You will need a good working knowledge of all the tools, particularly fill flash, GND, and manual camera controls. If you master these tools you will be free to make photos that tell at a glance the story about the place. Once published, you will have given the viewer a sense of this distant place and a reason to go there.

Point of View

Vary your lens use and give your photos of icons a unique touch. Shoot from a high angle, from below, from a good distance away, and shoot very tight. Strive to make photos that are somehow unique and different even when the places in your photos are well known.

This is where your interchangeable lenses or zoom lenses can bring variety. Where your 200 and 300 mm lenses can compress space and where your GND and steadying techniques can bring you the difficult and unusual shots. Consider interior scenes, twilight photos, the city at night; make the kinds of photos that show well-known places in a new light.

If your photos are somehow different than all the rest you will have sales. Most people will not bother with a beanbag or tripod; they will not learn to use fill-flash or learn to use the GND, they will not photograph at dawn or at dusk. If you master the tools your photos are sure to rise above the pack.

Captions

Carefully caption each photo but avoid empty adjectives like pretty and beautiful, awesome and amazing. Answer the who, what, when, where, why and how of journalism.

Notes, Tape Recorder

You will have your reward later if you take good notes while out photographing in a distant land; every photograph that you try to sell will have as part of its value a strong caption.

The caption should at least tell the journalistic who, what, when, where, why and how.

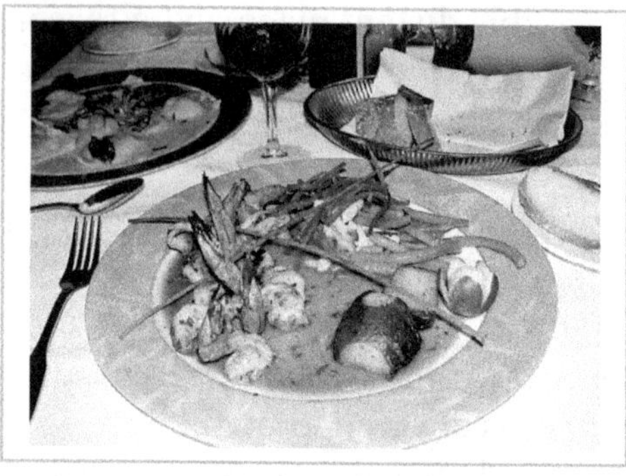

New York City's Little Italy features over 30 Italian restaurants on Mulberry Street.

Correct Spelling

Correct spelling is crucial, especially of proper names. You may not be able to return to a place soon and it could cost you much time and effort to look up the correct spelling.

Accurate description and correct spelling will be part of your reputation when sending photos out for publication. The more accurately you can create captions at the location, the better will be your believability as a photographer.

Use a tape recorder or a notebook to get the spelling of names correct. Photograph signs and maps if need be. Write notes and then make a digital photo of the notes to accompany your image files.

Record the details accurately and you will be thankful that you did when you later package up your files for a photo feature for a web magazine or put together images for a stock photo agency.

A digital photograph of a map could aid later in making captions by providing proper spelling of place names.

The caption will be equally important to all your photos especially photos that you submit to a stock agency because stock photos are sold by keyword and caption; the buyer will search for the appropriate photo by keyword and caption.

Take maps from tourist bureaus and agencies; travel editors will request that you send them maps with your articles or photo features.

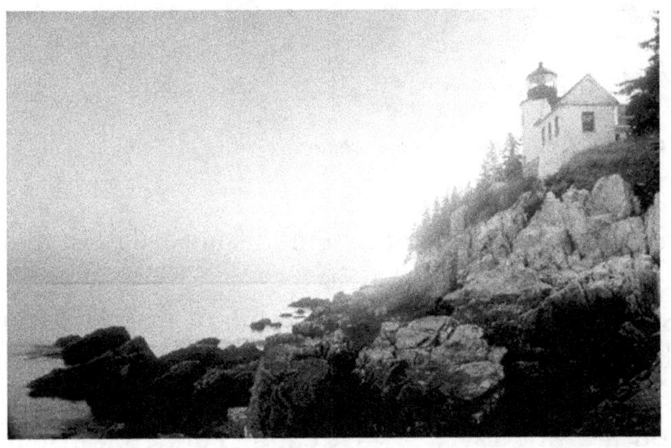

Bass Harbor Head Lighthouse, built in 1858 on the southwest side of Maine's Mount Desert Island, guides shipping on Penobscot Bay from 56 feet above sea level in Acadia National Park. A walkway to the sea beside the light affords access for photographs.

Here you give the editor plenty of information for their editing, cutting, or including

Icons

Include sites or monuments that have made the location famous and include vignettes of flowers or foods if the region you are covering is well known for that icon. The same holds true for covered bridges, lobster dinners, lighthouses, vineyards, and archaeological ruin sites.

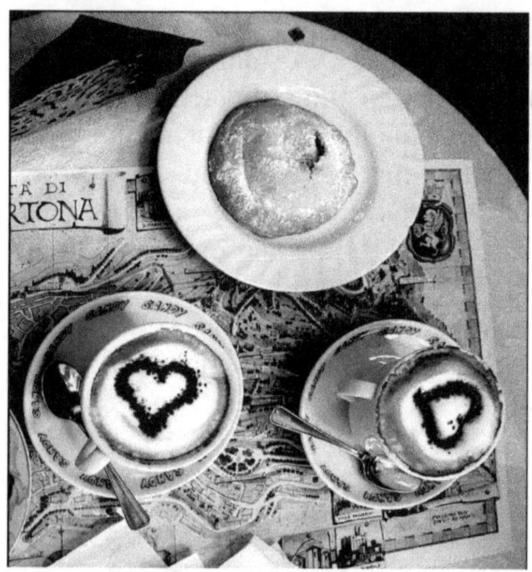

Map of Cortona, Italy Photo by Rain Rodolph

If you are covering the State of Maine, for instance, you will want a close-up photo of lobsters. Why not make it unusual by showing a group of vacationers eating a lobster dinner. Take it further by showing the distant islands and a fishing village.

This is where your mastery of depth of field will come into play. Include the foreground, mid ground, and background; make your photos tell the complete story.

If you are at New York's Central Park, for instance, and you want a tight shot of flowers, why not combine the iconic city background and the flowers while at the same time including people in your photos. You could, for instance, photograph groups of people walking through the park from a low angle with flowers in the foreground and the skyline in the background.

Every vacation spot has its special foods like the Maine lobster, the New Orleans beignet, and the Maryland crab cake. Markets both rural and urban can produce photos of places that people like to visit when they are vacationing.

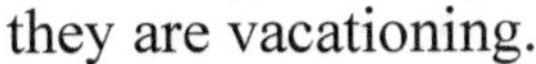

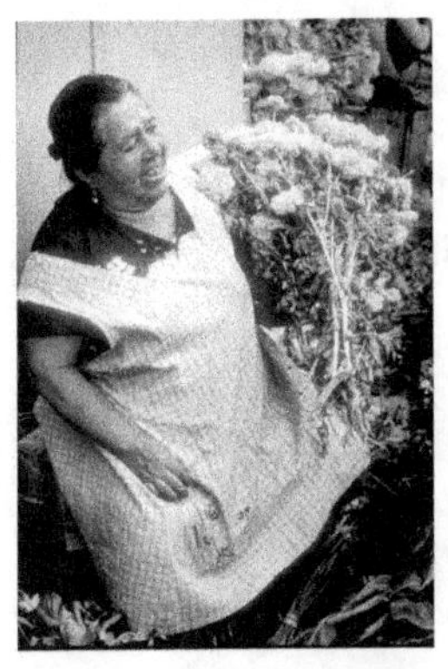

Shopping tops many vacationer's list of activities particularly in the exotic markets of distant cultures or where local artisans produce unique art. All of these places will bring their photo challenges. To add challenge, you will be on the move, setting shutter speed, focus, and exposure; you will need to practice with these tools of the travel photographer ahead of your vacation to gain familiarity with your camera and its tools.

And while you are at it don't forget the most sought after icon, romance.

Romance

Capture the feeling of romance and the feeling of freedom on resort beaches by making low light photos at sunset. Use the graduated neutral density filter to balance the bright sky and use a tripod, a beanbag, or other support to steady the camera.

Pre-focus your manual camera for maximum depth of field, attach your GND to balance the sky, set your camera's timer to overcome vibration and give yourself time to get in position, press the button and jump in the scene with your partner; put it all together for a romantic icon and an easy model release.

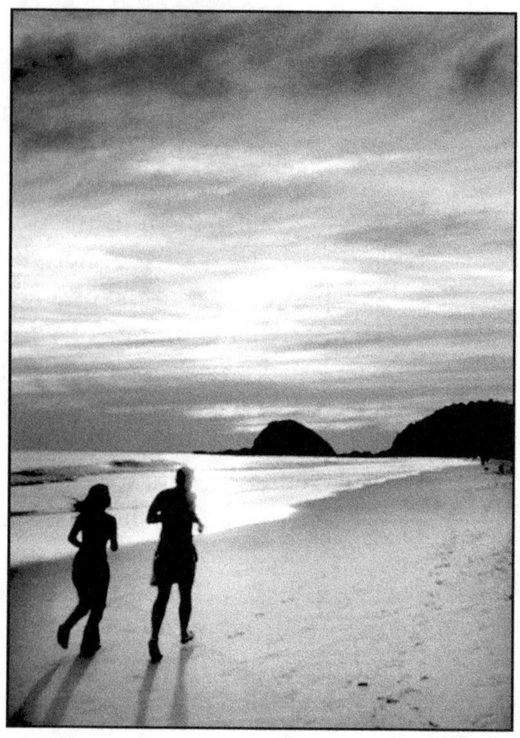

Romance can make a marketable photo and might be easy to create while on a beach vacation in the tropics. Camera steadying technique will come into play here along with balancing of the exposure.

Put It All Together

In this sunset beach scene, a beanbag propped on a table steadied the camera while the ten-second timer tripped the shutter. The camera was set to properly expose the foreground while a three-stop graduated neutral density filter with the dark portion rotated over the top half of the lens prevented the sky from loosing detail due to an over exposure.

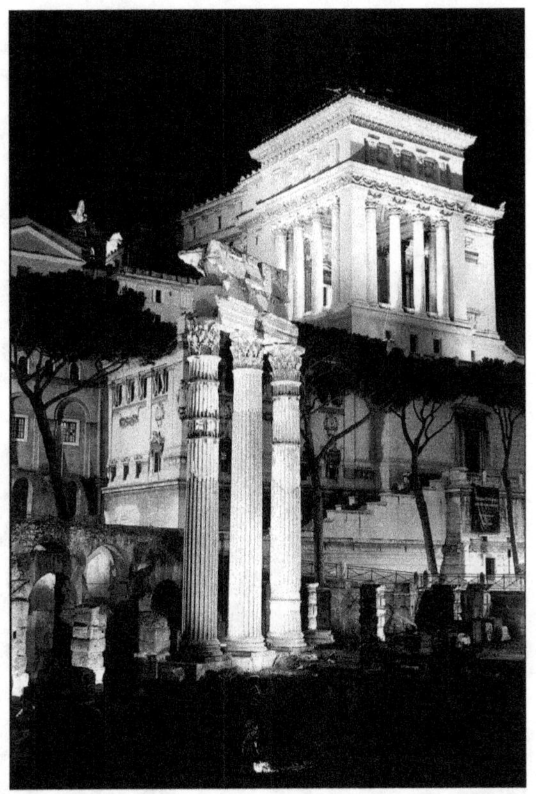

Night scenes can add interest to a photo feature and will involve all your tools. The photographer made this scene of a ruin in Rome while the camera was on a tripod. The exposure was four seconds.

Here you read the light with your camera's meter, then pre-set the shutter speed, manually focus the lens using hyperfocal distance technique, (Chapter 7) and use the timer to give the camera a chance to settle. On an extended exposure, you will want to remain still so as not to shake the ground while the lens is open.

The digital camera makes shots like this possible because you can review and change your settings until you achieve the desired result.

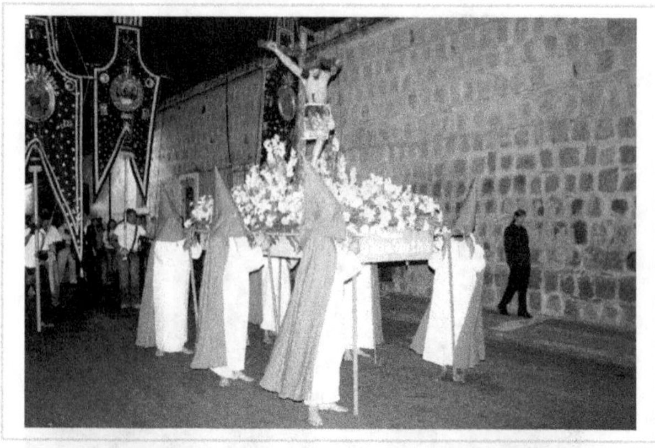

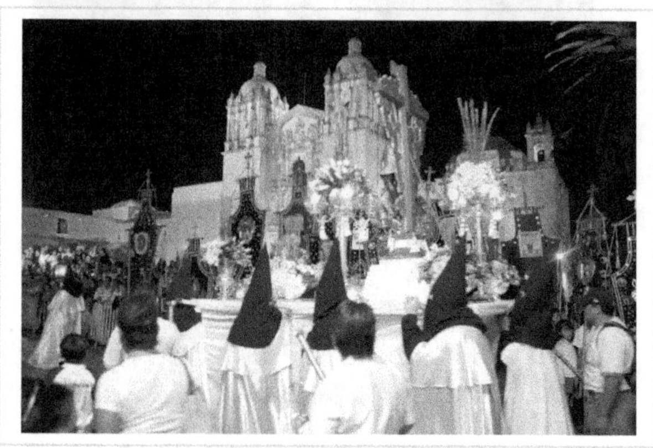

Twilight street scenes like this religious festival require steadying techniques or the use of a tripod.

Traveling With Digital Equipment

In the following chapter we look at traveling with digital equipment and how to get your digital photo equipment to a distant destination safely.

Modern Photography: The Collodion Process introduced in 1851 by London sculptor Frederick Scott Archer allowed exposure times of seconds and ushered in the age of modern photography.

Chapter Five, Traveling With Digital Equipment

For the traveling digital photographer, the storage of images and the power needs of the camera will require the packing of some special electronic equipment.

Power Supply

First on the list will be the power supply at the destination. Is it the same as your home country or do you need an adapter and a converter? (*See Chart Next Page for a Partial list*)

Check this website for a complete list of countries and their power systems *http://kropla.com/electric2.htm*

You will find that very few hotels in the world have ample power outlets and therefore it is prudent to bring a power strip with multiple outlets, preferable one with built-in surge suppression.

You will power up camera battery chargers, possibly a computer, and perhaps a battery charger for a flash unit. You will need multiple power outlets.

If you are traveling with companions, the fight for the hotel outlets could get testy.

Power Supply Worldwide:

Africa, South: 220 Volts
Australia: 220-240 V
China: 220 V 50 Hz
US and Canada: 110, Volts Flat two pin
France: 110 -220 Volts Round pin
Great Britain: 230 V 50 Hz Square pin
India: 230-340 Volts 50 cycles, power surges common
Italy, Germany, (European Union) Varies within the country.
Japan: 100 volt ac 50 or 60 cycles depending on region
Korea: 220 V 60 Hz
Mexico: 120 Volts, 60 Hz Similar to US and Canada
New Zealand: 230 Volts 50 Hz
Russia: 220 V 50 Hz
Spain 230 : Volts 50 Hz
South America: Ecudor110 volt,
Bolivia: 110 and 220 volt,
Peru: 110 and 220 volt

From this representative list you can see that there are many differences throughout the world.

See a full List ***http://kropla.com/electric2.htm***

Adapter, Converters, Power Stabilizers

The trick to traveling and meeting your power needs in a country foreign to you is to find the adapter, the converter, and, in some cases of a long-term stay, the power stabilizer, that will allow you to safely plug in your devices.

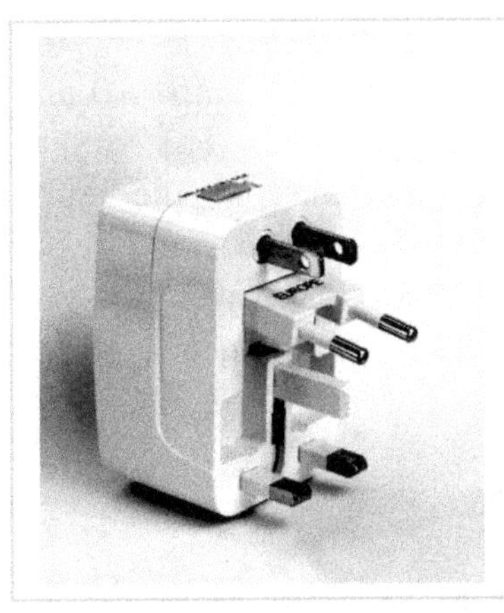

The universal plug adapter will allow you to plug in electrical devices in Europe and the Americas.

The Adapter allows you to change the shape of the plug-in, going from the two-prong, flat-pin of the US, Canada, and Mexico, for instance, to the round pin type of Europe.

The Converter changes the voltage. A good example is plugging in to the French 220 volts and converting it to the 110 volts used by the US, Mexico, and Canada. *(Your computer battery charger is likely designed to work on 110 or 220 voltage and 50 or 60 cycles. Check the label to be sure)*

The Stabilizer does just that, it keeps the voltage even. In tropical locations, for example, there are occasional power outages, power surges, and power drops, particularly on the hot afternoons when air conditioners tax the power system. A stabilizer protects your equipment from drops and surges in voltage. With its built-in battery it allows you to safely shut down equipment after a power outage.

Surge Protector

The surge protector is a common device often built into a power strip. This will protect your equipment during a power surge or lightning storm. The surge protector offers only limited protection, however; you should unplug your devices during electrical storms and when you are not using them.

When in doubt about the power supply, ask.

Several of the countries listed above use both 110 and 220 volt system depending on the region. The city of Paris uses both 110 and 220, at times in the same building.

Once you have your power needs taken care of, you next need to consider where to store your images.

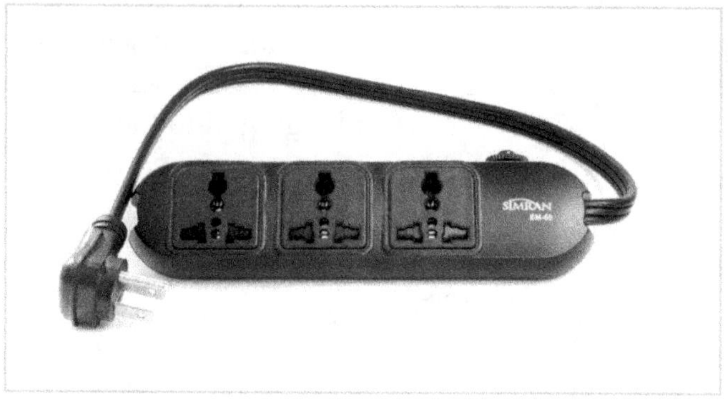

The Universal power strip with three receptacles designed to accept European and North American plugs. The device also has a built-in surge suppressor.

Digital Image Storage

A 12-megapixel camera will produce a file of about twenty three megabytes for each photo when shot at a high-quality capture mode such as RAW. If you convert these files to 8"x 12" x 300 dpi TIFF while on the road, you could have a 25-80 megabyte file for each image after conversion from Raw format to TIFF.

(You should also save the RAW file for your archive.)

There will be no avoiding it; the need for storage will become critical.

If your working mode would be to convert your images from RAW to TIFF while on the road to then do a final clean up before sending them to an editor, you would need lots of storage space.

(More about archiving and delivering Raw and TIFF in Chapter 6)

Laptop Image Storage

If you travel with a laptop or notebook, you can load and store the files in the computer's hard drive or store the files on a portable image storage system.

Attempting to store images on memory discs or CF cards would not be practical as you will have too many images.

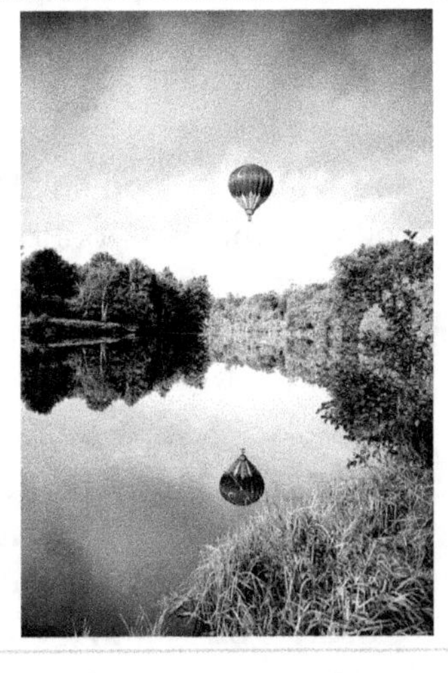

For location photos bring a compass so that you know where the sun will rise and set. Check the wind; morning photos on water will usually give the best reflections.

The best storage option is the remote hard drive. They are small and not too expensive at $100.00 USD for a remote hard drive with several hundred gigabyte or even two terabyte capacity.

Lacie and Seagate make a good range of remote hard drives that are robust enough to travel. There are other storage devices made just for the purpose, some with a small viewing screen so that you can be sure that you were successful in storing your images before you reformat your camera's CF memory card.

DVD Burner

Although the CD and DVD were once good storage options they are not as nimble as a remote hard drive. Burning the images to a DVD takes time and retrieving the images once you return home takes even more of your time. Other issues such as the archival quality of CDs and DVDs, and the fact that many laptops no longer come equipped with a burner installed have diminished the value of the CD/DVD as a storage system.

The various upload cloud systems of storage are also in doubt because of the difficulty of finding reliable web service when traveling and the time it takes to upload files. The upload systems could be of value for unique images but are difficult to use for mass storage.

Remote Hard Drive

With fast storage speeds, enormous capacity, and small size, the remote hard drive has become the best option while traveling. Images store quickly in folders labeled with place names and you can find and retrieve them quickly.

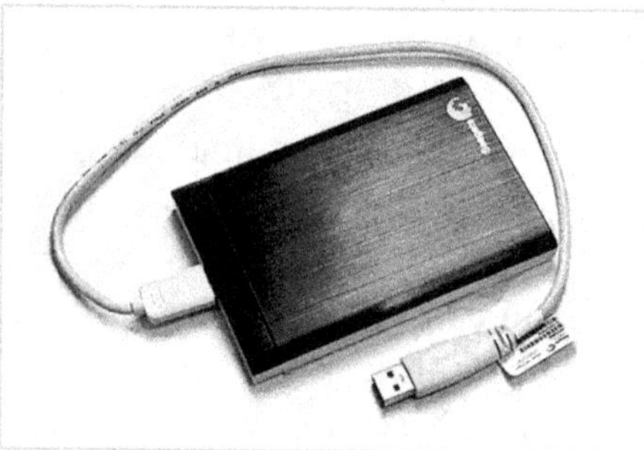

The remote hard drive with a capacity of two terabytes of storage (2000 gigabytes) for less than $100.00 USD will give ample image storage of photos and video for several weeks of vacation

You can store unique images and those that you worked hard to make on both the laptop and the remote hard drive for backup. Some photographers will carry two hard drives and archive images in three places just to be safe.

Battery Charger

The battery charger for the camera and an extra battery will round out the digital tool kit and although the digital photographer doesn't lug film, with the storage and battery needs, the load gets a little more complicated than for the film-based photographer.

Airports, X-rays, and Metal Detectors

The digital photographer will encounter two difficulties at the airport: the metal detector and the X-ray.

Your laptop and hard drives should go through the x-ray machine along with your carry-on luggage.

Although hard drives could go into checked luggage where they will receive x-ray inspection which should not harm them, they will receive rough treatment (extremely rough) and an inspection by airport luggage handlers who might open your luggage. Laptops, cameras, portable hard drives, and jump drives are better off traveling in carry-on luggage and being passed through the X-ray machine.

See the Transportation Security Administration guidelines on the web at, ***www.tsa.gov*** for info on US flights.

Your laptop and portable hard drives should not go through the metal detector because, according to most experts, the metal detectors could cause damage to the information on the hard drive.

Film, regardless whether it is exposed or not exposed, (before processing or development) should be hand inspected if possible and not passed through the X-ray.

The current TSA guideline is that film below 800 ISO can withstand five X-rays before damage occurs. No problem with low speed film but many international flights could include three or four connections and passes through the X-ray. A round trip, international flight could easily involve trips through five X-ray inspections. Best to ask for a hand inspection of film to try to minimize the number of times your film goes through X-ray.

Film should not go into checked luggage because it could receive a high dose of X-ray that might fog the film.

You are best to carry film in a clear plastic bag for easy hand inspection. The TSA guidelines do allow for hand inspection of pushed or underexposed film and films for special processing.

Getting your images home from a trip by air is not always easy but with one or two small hard-drive storage systems in place and perhaps a cloud system or upload to your own website for the unique images, you should get through security with no loss of your photos.

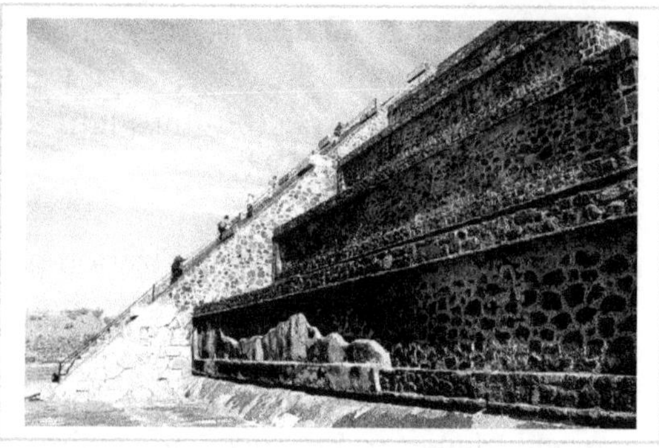

The people climbing the Pyramid of the Moon at Teotihuacan in Mexico give the structure scale. Here the camera is set low to the ground to make the structure appear even larger than it is

The next chapter looks at image capture and image storage, two of the traveling digital photographer's enduring challenges.

In 1853 Frenchman Gaspar Felix Tournachon outfitted his hot air balloon with a darkroom and made wet plate aerial photographs.

Chapter Six, Image Format

The Digital Image Format

Creating photos for sale while traveling will require that you plan well a format for the storage of your images. Not just for the immediate storage of images while on vacation but a format that allows you to build an archive of your images for sale long into the future.

The following chapter will detail image capture and the image formats that you will need to consider when making travel photos and when preparing them for delivery to a photo editor

RAW, TIFF, JPEG

You will have three common formats to work with when preparing images for publication: RAW, TIFF, and JPEG.

Image Size

In order to have widely marketable images you will need to capture the largest possible and best quality image your camera can produce. Raw capture in 12 to 16-bit mode is the best method of capture available and will result in the best image file. If your camera doesn't have the raw feature, make the largest possible file size that your camera will record.

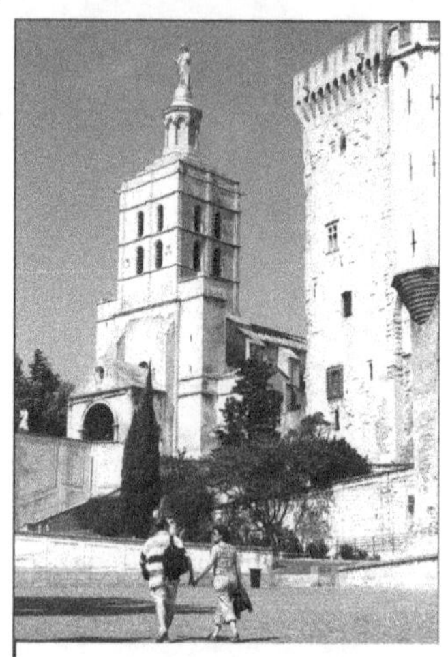

This building in Provence has been there since the 14th Century. Your photo of it could sell for years to come if you archive it properly

Why Raw Capture

Raw capture will produce for you an archive of photos that you can work with and improve long into the future for repeat and continued sales.

Most digital SLR cameras will offer a raw capture option and you should use this option to capture your images.

Raw capture will produce 12 to 16 bit, unsharpened files that contain all the potential of your camera. These files allow you to make photos for publication, photos that could be enlarged for posters, book covers, textbook illustrations, and a dozen other applications in the commercial realm where the buyers prefer large files.

Each brand of cameras uses its own format, generically called raw. Canon, for example, uses CR2 format. These files are can be considered your digital negatives and they can be converted into quite large TIFFs and JPEGs while still retaining their quality.

Don't be misled by the great look of a small-file, jpeg web image on the computer screen; these images are displaying at 72 pixels per inch and will not stand up to enlargement for printing in a magazine or enlarging for a web magazine. You must make large files to create photos suitable for publication in a print magazine, web magazine, or placement with a stock agency.

Stock agencies want images that have wide sales potential. The standard file size for a stock agency could be as large as 13 inches by 19 inches by 300 pixels per inch. A magazine purchasing rights from you or from your stock agency might require images that are minimum 8 inches by 12 inches by 300 pixels per inch. A raw file can handle that conversion, a small jpeg can not.

Raw capture produces a relatively small file compared to a Tiff and therefore makes an ideal capture and archive system for the traveling photographer faced with limited storage capacity. Not only is the raw file size relatively small, but raw capture offers the potential of sales to the broadest possible markets and sales well into the future as you improve that image in post-production software.

Although you might have one market in mind when you create the image, a newspaper that would be happy with a small jpeg for instance, if you capture the image in JPEG format at a low resolution you have limited the potential of that image.

The image that you thought would have limited value often draws more sales than you expected. Therefore you should give all of your images their best chance of longevity and repeat sales to the broadest possible markets.

You might later want to offer your images to a stock photography agency or a print magazine. If you capture in raw and save the images as shot, they become your digital archive images and will have unlimited potential. You can always make a TIFF for publication or a small

JPEG for the web from your raw image file; going down in size is easy but going up in size is next to impossible.

Control

Other strengths of raw capture are the ease with which you can process the image and the degree of control that raw capture gives you.

In raw capture the camera does little to the image, it renders just the way that you shot it. You make any needed adjustments in the software that came with your camera when you convert the image. (disable sharpening) You adjust white balance and exposure, levels and saturation, and you do this on a copy while saving the original raw file as you would a negative in its unaltered state.

You can use the pristine digital raw image in many forms and sell it many times into the future. You can apply new techniques as you master them and as new software innovations are developed. With a TIFF file you have slightly limited the potential of the image once you have converted it from raw to TIFF. Even worse is the limit of potential if you have captured the image as a small Jpeg.

Bit Depth

Bit depth determines the degree of detail of an image, particularly in the dark and light areas, and it determines the levels of subtlety in tone transition.

Your camera might have options for you to set when you capture images. The options range from the highest level, 12 or 16-bit raw, an unaltered file that has all the levels of brightness available, to the other end of the scale, the 8-bit jpeg, a smaller file with limited levels of brightness.

The higher the bit depth, 12, 14, or 16, the more subtlety an image will have in its tone transition and the more detail it will have in its dark and light areas and the better it will tolerate computer improvements.

For many publications this degree of subtlety will be of no consequence but, in order for you to have all markets open to your submissions, you should capture and archive in raw at the highest available bit depth.

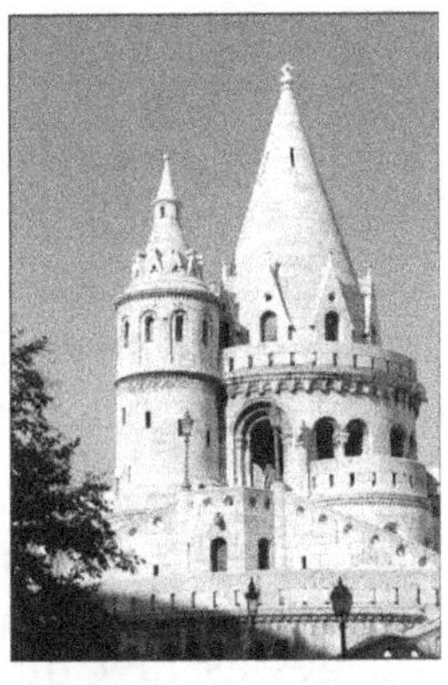

Budapest, Hungary Photo, Rain Rodolph
With exotic buildings like this to photograph, saving and storing images while traveling will be one of the digital photographers biggest challenges.

Potential of Digital Negatives

If you create your images in raw at 16-bit and save the unaltered file as you would a negative, you will have at your disposal the best negative available and you will have unlimited potential for sales. There is just more clean information to work with in 12 or 16-bit, RAW capture and it is about potential: potential to improve the image as your technique improves and the potential to make sales in unlimited markets.

Disable Sharpening.

One of the great things about raw capture is that the camera is not allowed to change the image in any way. Raw will not include sharpening, a step that can be particularly damaging to an image if done carelessly or done as a first step. Sharpening (and unsharp mask) should be done as a last step and done by the photo editor. Editors will request that you do no sharpening. They want to have their people perform the sharpening as a last step.

If you are not using raw you should go into your camera's menu and disable sharpening if possible. Failing that; set the camera's sharpening to the lowest possible number.

Raw File Size

Another great feature about raw capture is that the file sizes are small when compared to a TIFF, while at the same time they have all the information that the camera captured.

Working with a raw copy in the software that comes with your camera, you can make many adjustments to the image without damaging it. In TIFF format at 16 bits you can make further adjustments if needed. Once you have the image prepared then you reduce it to 8-bit, convert it to TIFF or jpeg depending on the editor's request, and you send it to the editor.

Digital Negative: Raw

As mentioned, if you store your images as raw files and treat those files as your negatives, that is, you do little to change them as you would a film negative, you will have archived your images in the most efficient way for later use. And you never know what that use might be. Your unusual images could sell many times for you over the years if you have archived the file as a raw negative.

Once you return from a trip, make a copy of the raw files and store the originals away, perhaps on a remote hard drive at a relative's house. You then can make changes to the copies of the raw files while preserving the originals.

There is no predicting what new software and new techniques will develop. With your digital negatives, you can extend the marketable life of your images.

For additional detailed information check out this website: ***www.updig.org***

UPDIG is a convention developed by a consortium of industry professionals who have attempted to standardize the creating, transporting, and publishing of digital images for photographers and editors. (Free download) You can follow the UPDIG guidelines to stay up to date with changes.

Color Space

Most digital cameras will give you an option of choosing a color space. Adobe RGB is the standard and you should set up your camera and your computer to produce images in that color system (color space) because it is compatible with the editor's requirements and those of the printers that will reproduce your photos in magazines and newspapers.

Color space refers to the many systems that digital devices use to represent and reproduce color. The color space that your camera and computer uses could determine the quality of the reproduction.

Three color spaces will be of concern to the digital photographer who intends to publish:

- RGB (Adobe RGB)
- CYMK
- sRGB

RGB

RGB refers to the three basic colors that the computer monitor uses to reproduce color: **R**ed, **G**reen, and **B**lue.

Scanners, digital cameras, and television monitors also use RGB as a system of reproducing color.

The monitors use light shining through colored filters that mix at various intensities to produce a wide range of colors. When no light is present, we see black on the computer screen, when the device adds the three colors at full intensity, we see white, and when the device adds colors in equal parts at medium intensity, we see gray. If this medium intensity is not exactly equal, and we have a bit more intensity of one of the three colors, we will see gray with a slight color cast or hue. It is the intensity and the amount of color that the device blends or adds that determines the ultimate color.

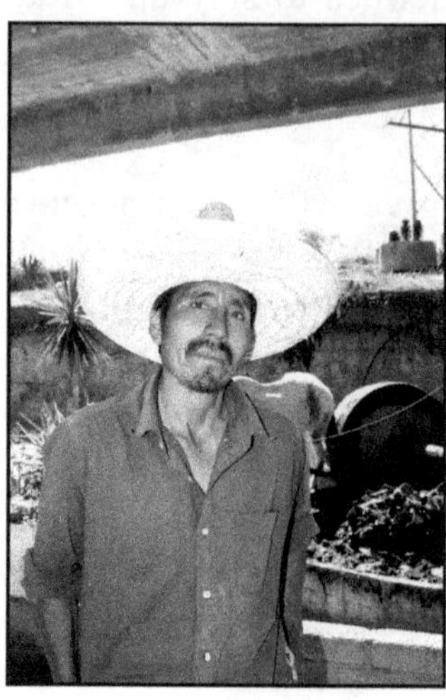

You would not want to go through the work of using fill flash to brighten the face under the wide brimmed hat and the GND to balance exposure only to find that you had created the images as too small a jpeg or that you sent them to the editor too small for printing.

Calibrate Monitor

RGB depends solely on a device, that is the camera, the computer monitor, or the scanner, to render a given color. For this reason, you should calibrate your computer monitor and scanner and you should make sure that your camera's white balance is properly set for the ambient conditions in which you photograph. Most cameras will have an automatic white balance feature.

Scanners and CRT monitors need occasional calibrating because the bulbs and tubes change with age.

If you are using a cathode ray tube monitor, (CRT) you should calibrate it every few months (*they change with age*) so that what you see for color on the screen is truer to the standard and that your gray tones are truly neutral gray.

If you are using Adobe products, you should see in your computer's control panel an Adobe Gamma setting for calibrating your monitor.

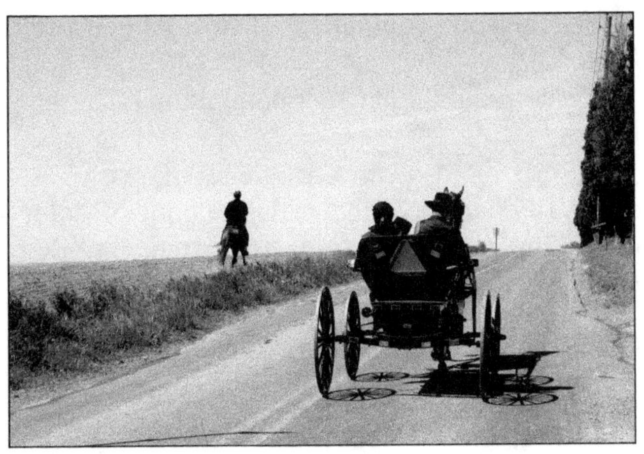

Set the color space of your camera and your computer to be compatible with the editor's color space, Adobe RGB or Adobe RGB 1998. Use the UPDIG recommendations and hope that the editor and the print house are using the same guidelines.

Computer Color Space

It is important that you set your computer and camera color space to RGB, the industry standard and the color space that most photo editors will use both on Mac and PC.

Look for the place to set this in your photo imaging software, and also in your camera menu where it could be listed as Adobe RGB. Your choices in your camera might be limited to sRGB and Adobe RGB. Set the camera for Adobe RGB; it will give you a wider gamut of colors to work with. Most editors will be working in the Adobe RGB color space.

Free Download:

If you have Adobe programs you will already have Adobe 1998 on your computer. If not, Adobe offers a free download:

www.adobe.com/digitalimag/adobergb.html

Adobe RGB is a very specific RGB color space designed in 1998 to have the widest gamut of color for working on images and to closely match CYMK, the other color space of most concern to photographers who would publish their work.

CYMK

This color space refers to the colors **C**yan, **Y**ellow, **M**agenta, and black, **K**, colors that a printer uses when it sprays ink on paper. These inks overlap and blend on the paper and create many intensities of color.

Unlike RGB, the colors are not activated by a light shining through filters to the observer, but by reflected light that bounces back to the observer from ink on a surface. These colors absorb light or subtract light.

Editors rarely ask you to send images in CYMK; the print house will make the conversion from RGB to CYMK in the pre-press phase.

When you work with your home digital printer to make ink-jet prints, you will work on the images in RGB which the printer will automatically convert to CYMK. You should do your work on digital images in the computer in RGB (Adobe RGB 1998) and you should send the images to the editor in RGB if sending TIFF files. Leave it up to the editor or print house to convert the images to CMYK just before they print them.

When you convert your images to jpeg for sending to the editor, the jpeg conversion should be set to preserve the RGB color space.

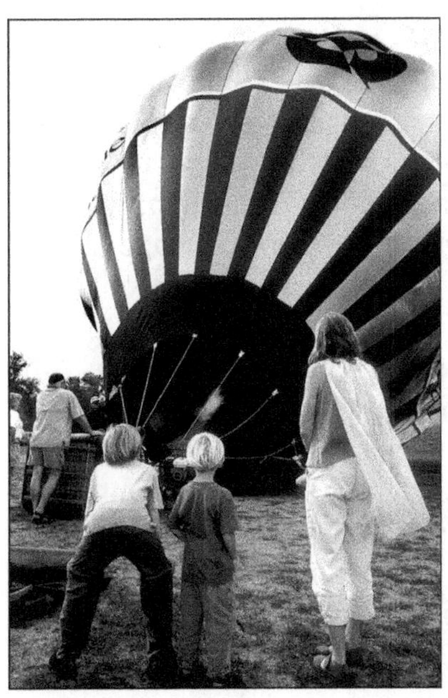

Capture images at 100 ISO in RAW or high JPEG.
Set up the camera to capture in RGB (Adobe RGB 1998)

sRGB

The third color space of concern to the photographer is sRGB, a small gamut color space (small range of colors) developed for the web.

This color space is commonly used for small files sent over the web in emails or for web pages. Its small gamut (range of colors) was designed to allow web pages to rapidly download and to match the computer monitor which, at 72 pixels per inch, has a much smaller gamut than the CYMK printing that a magazine will do.

The gamut (number or range of colors) of sRGB is smaller than Adobe RGB 1998 and therefore, the photographer creating images for sale should not use sRGB in digital capture. Nor should sRGB be used in preparing images for later high quality CYMK printing unless the editor requests sRGB.

Your camera may have an sRGB capture option but you should not use it to make photos that you intend to print or that you will send to a magazine. The camera's sRGB option is there for those that will make small files for sending over the internet and displaying on a computer's 72 pixel per inch monitor.

More About Adobe RGB 1998

This color space was created by Adobe in 1998 to come close to matching colors available in CYMK.

You can set your computer software to work in this color space. If you are using Adobe Photoshop, you can activate the option that warns you when an image has no imbedded color space or when the color space is not Adobe 1998.

Find this in Photoshop under edit, color settings. In the settings option, click on North American Pre-press 2, and the proper settings for preparing images for printing should be active including the checks for a warning when you open an image without a color profile. (color space) This will warn you if you are capturing in the wrong color space or if you are converting images without preserving the color space.

Color Space

Color space is more an issue with high quality reproduction such as you will find in glossy magazines, calendars, posters, and the like. It is less a concern to editors using small jpegs, but you should preserve the RGB color space when sending files to an editor.

The next chapter looks at the details: depth of field, exposure, and focus: technical considerations important to your ability to make consistently marketable travel photos.

British Photographer Roger Fenton (1819-1869), one of the earliest war photographers, documented the Crimean War in 1855 using a horse-drawn darkroom.

Chapter Seven, Minding The Details

Camera Technique:

This chapter goes into a little advanced camera technique. You don't need to master all the techniques to make marketable photos but the more technical expertise you acquire, the easier it will be to fill a photo editors needs.

Sharp Focus

The ability to make sharply focused photos will be critical to your success. Although you will see selectively focused photos and blurred photos in publication, a portfolio full of these photos will be hard to sell to a broad market.

Depth of Field

This term describes the area within a photograph that is in sharp focus. The following are some of the most frequently asked questions about depth of field.

Q. *How does the aperture setting determine depth of field?*

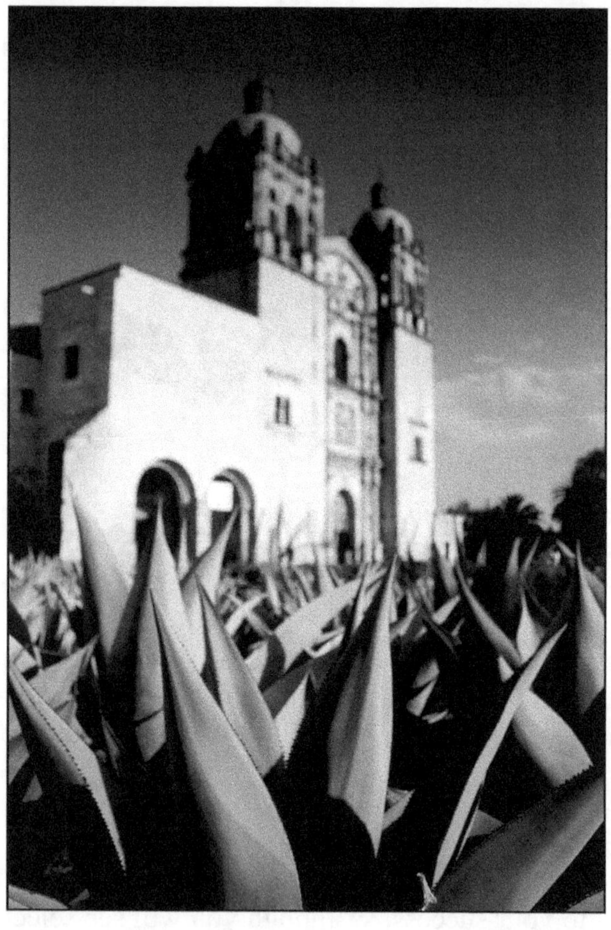

In this photo the aperture was set at f-3.5 and the shutter speed was set to 1/2000 of a second. The focus point was about six feet in front of the camera.

A. An aperture wide-open, such as f-3.5, will result in a photo having a very limited area of sharpness, as the photo above demonstrates. The church steeple is not in focus while the plants in the foreground are sharply focused.

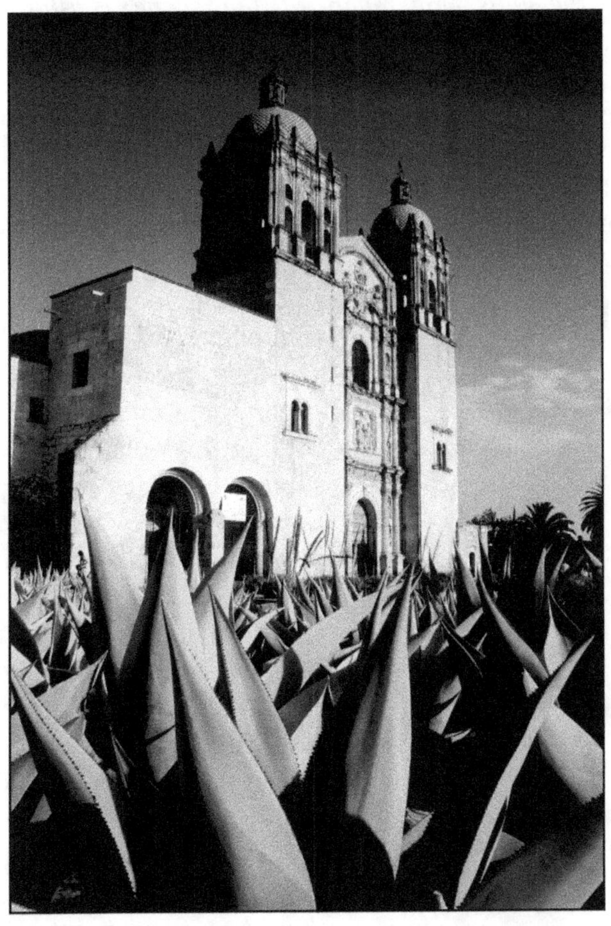

In this photo, the aperture was set to f-22 and the shutter speed went to1/60 of a second. The focus point remained the same, about six feet in front of the camera.

The smallest aperture or opening of the lens diaphragm will result in the greatest depth of field. This means that the largest number on the lens scale, usually f-22 or f-32, will result in more of the photo being in sharp focus.

Q. *Why is it that with the aperture set at f-22 when I look through the lens not much of the scene is sharply-focused?*

A. When you look through the lens, you are looking through a wide-open aperture. Once you press the shutter button, the aperture mechanism instantly closes down and the light reflecting from the subject comes through the small opening in the center of the lens to the sensor or film plane.

Many books and web pages are available with detailed information on the subject of optics and hyper focal distance but when starting out it is enough to remember that the largest aperture number will give you the smallest opening in your aperture and this will result in the maximum area of sharpness in your photo.

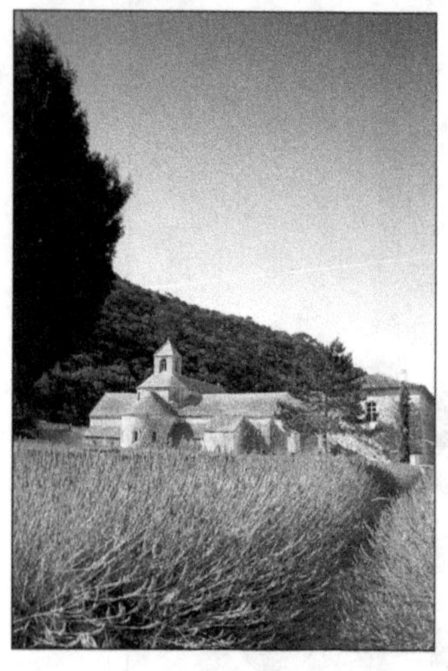

To get sharpness throughout in these Provence lavender fields, the aperture was set to f-22 and the shutter speed to 1/30 of a second. The camera was on a tripod and the focus point was just 10 feet in front of the camera

Q. *To get the most depth of field sharpness, where should my focus point be?*

A. One popular rule of thumb and a good place to start out is the, "One Third/Two Thirds Rule."

While this rule will not cover all situations, particularly in landscapes, start with it as you develop your focusing skills and bring much more of the foreground into focus.

As you have noticed, when you look through the lens before taking the photo you see only a small portion of the frame sharply focused. To gain maximum depth of sharpness you must go to manual focus, if possible, and focus the lens at a point one-third into the distance of the frame. This will give you improved sharpness in the foreground while retaining background focus when the aperture closes down at the press of the shutter. This rule of thumb will result in a larger area of sharpness in the frame and is a handy rule to remember while photographing on the move.

This rule, however, applies mainly to close-ups; for landscapes, there is a better method to enhance depth of field.

Focus

In cameras with fixed focal length lenses, (non zoom) the distance between the near focal point and a sharply focused infinity is relatively easy to set by using the depth of field marks on the film barrel and setting a zone of focus. With zoom lenses, however, the task becomes more difficult and with many digital lenses you may have no marks at all on the lens barrel to aid in focusing.

By using the one-third/two-third rule with any lens you can gain some sharpness in the foreground.

When using an automatically focusing lens you can get your focus point one-third into the frame and then lock the focus in place. (depress the shutter button partially in some cameras, shut off auto focus in others) Once the focus is locked, aim the camera to include the entire scene. (set up your camera to work in this mode)

This will gain a little more foreground sharpness and while helpful, this rule is more appropriate for close-ups and less than perfect in landscapes; you can do better.

Hyperfocal Distance

You can refine your depth of field technique even further by determining the hyperfocal distance of your lens. Gain a few more feet of foreground sharpness by using hyperfocal distance focusing techniques.

The commonly used definition for hyperfocal distance describes it as the closest distance at which the lens can be focused while at the same time keeping objects at infinity sharp,

This means that by focusing the lens, when it is wide open, to a point very near the camera, you will move the area of sharpness closer to the camera while still keeping the area beyond this focusing point sharp. (You must have your aperture set at the high numbers and small openings, f-16, f-22, or f-32, to maximize this area of sharpness.)

The church photo on the previous page illustrates this; the focus point in both photos was about six feet in front of the camera at the leaf of the near plant.

For a 35 mm lens with the aperture set at f-22, the point of focus that will bring the most sharpness will be between 3 and 6 feet in front of the camera. For a 50 mm lens the focus point will be about 12 feet in front. These are approximate distances and could be even closer for various digital cameras. Each lens will be different. Lens specs and experimentation will help you find the hyperfocal distance for your lenses. Find this distance for each of your lenses beforehand.

A Leap Of Faith

These techniques take a bit of faith because when you look through the lens, there will be only a small portion of the frame in sharpness, the point of focus 6 to 12 feet in front of you. In the photo of the church, for instance, the only sharp area of the photo before the shutter was tripped was the plant six feet in front of the camera.

Keep in mind that when you have your camera set at a high f number such as f-22, and you press the shutter, the aperture mechanism will instantly close and cause the area from about one foot in front of you to the most distant object to be acceptably sharp.

Since the varying sizes of the digital sensors in the many camera models will make a difference in how the various cameras render depth of field you must test your camera. If you have a depth of field preview button on your camera you will see the effect of the closing aperture when you press the preview button. The darkening of the view screen, however, does make this difficult to see and it will take practice before you can make the depth of field preview button a useful tool.

Selective Focus:

The opposite of maximum depth is when you focus selectively, when you intentionally have one area of the photo in sharp focus while much of the rest of the frame is out of focus. To do this, use a small number aperture and this will give you a larger aperture opening, perhaps f-3.5 or f-4. These settings will result in a limited area of sharpness. Travel photography, however, will usually require maximum sharpness in the frame to tell a story about a place. You therefore will usually be striving for maximum depth of field by using the larger f numbers: f-16, f-22, or f-32.

Photos In Two Layers:

A digital camera opens up new techniques for achieving maximum depth of field and for creating evenly exposed frames. You can make sandwiched photos relatively easily and with little expense, other than time and lots of it spent on the computer.

Take two frames, each frame having a different level of depth of field. Create a photo with a sharply focused foreground and one with a sharply focused background and then combine them in the imaging software to create sharpness throughout.

You can also do a similar sandwich to create layered photos with a balanced exposure by properly exposing for the foreground in one frame and then exposing a second and perhaps third frame for the sky and combining the two in digital imaging software. *(HDR is a popular name for this technique, High Dynamic Range)*

While these techniques require lots of computer time and are considerably more work than using good camera technique, they do offer an alternate path. Keep in mind, however, that many photo editors and stock agencies will reject sandwiched photos when they are obviously manipulated or carelessly done. These photo techniques might also put the authenticity of your photos in doubt with some editors.

Balanced Exposure, GND, Fill Flash

Balancing your exposure is best done with the graduated neutral density filter and fill flash. (Chapter 3) Balance the exposure in the camera and also practice hyperfocal distance techniques to spare yourself hours spent on the computer. The best images are those made in the camera where you can achieve much better results with camera technique than you can achieve with a computer once you master the camera's tools.

Twilight Photos

Make interesting travel photos during the period after the sun has set but before night completely darkens the sky. Streetlights and cafe lights come on, the sky fills with afterglow, and with a little steadying of the camera, photos of interesting variety result.

Interior Photos

Restaurant interiors, clubs, and performance events can be interesting. The digital camera lets you correct for tungsten light's yellow tint and to balance other mixed lights either in the camera or in the computer.

Architectural Distortion

Buildings that appear to lean in towards each other result when we use wide-angle lenses. You can correct these in image editing software by using a distort tool or a

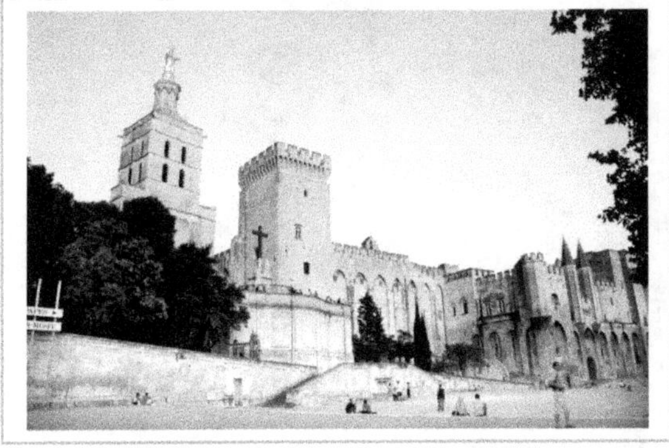

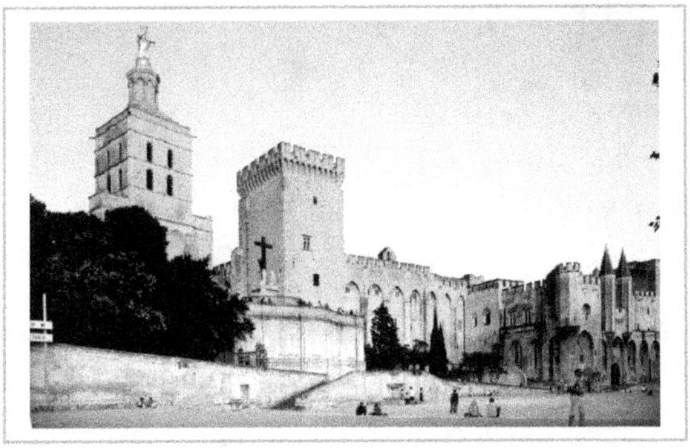

perspective correction tool. You could also step back and use a 50 mm lens or higher to avoid the leaning building look.

Some photo editors accept the look of leaning buildings, others do not. You can correct a few and leave others uncorrected in order to offer a variety of both styles when submitting photos for an editor's review.

Model Release

Ask your friends and family to model for you, the model release will be easy to obtain and many editors are looking for the everyday person not the posed model. See sample release forms in next chapter.

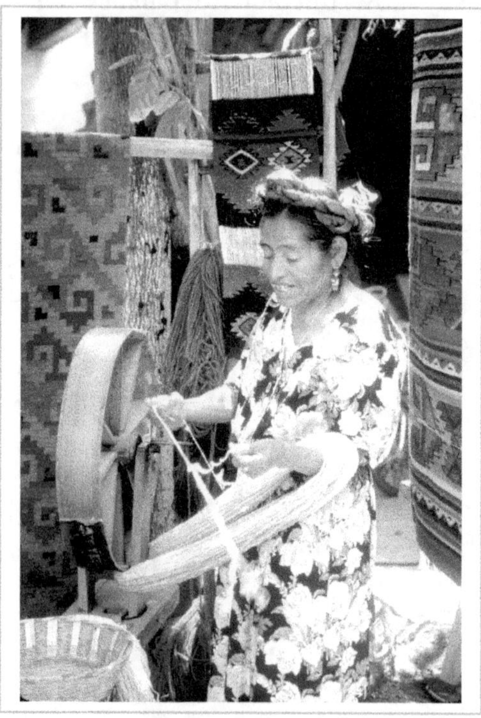

Offer your photos to artisans to make deeper coverage in a country foreign to you

People engaged in their trade might not mind posing for you if you offer something in return such as photos for an artisan's web site.

Ask recognizable people in your photos to sign a model release, the photo could bring sales through a stock agency if it has a model release.

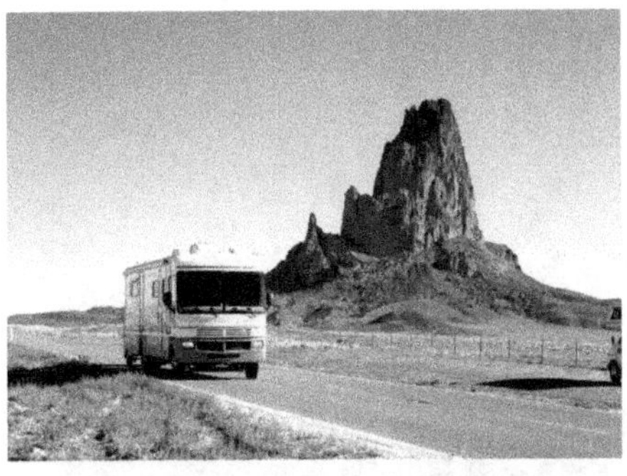

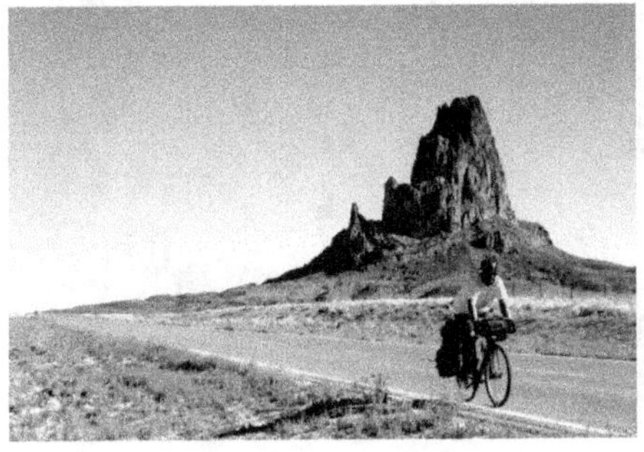

Find a good background and wait for appropriate action to help tell your travel story.

Create The Photo

Find the story telling background and pre-focus the lens, read the foreground, mid ground, and background, set the exposure, attach the GND and then wait. In the photos above the background sets the scene for a road trip story while the RV and then a long-distance biker tell two different road trip stories.

To make the balloon shot on the next page the photographer planned for this liftoff over the river by knowing the wind direction and the sun angle. Early morning brings little wind and good reflections on the water. The photo gives the reader the feeling that they could be in this scene enjoying the balloon ride. Action shots like this sell.

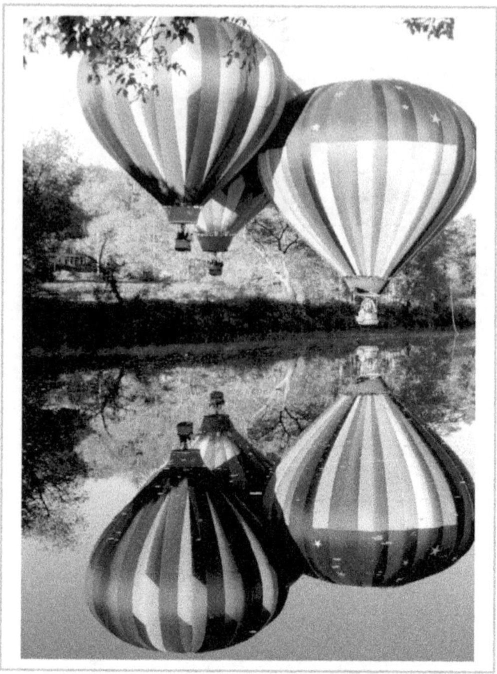

Photo: Jeanne McKenna

What Next

Once you have the digital equipment and the technique that will help you to make publishable photos, you must then learn a few skills needed to sell those photos.

Digital equipment has made this much easier than it ever was, particularly the ability to proof your work with the digital camera, to edit and size your work on the computer, and to make relatively inexpensive samples of your work to send to photo editors

Find The Editors

The following chapters detail techniques used to find and approach the editors who will buy your digital travel photos, a skill as important as your ability to make marketable photos.

In 1871, English Doctor Richard Maddox developed a method of using gelatin to make photographic plates thus introducing the dry plate process.

Make And Sell Digital Travel Photos

Part Two
Sell The Photos That You Create

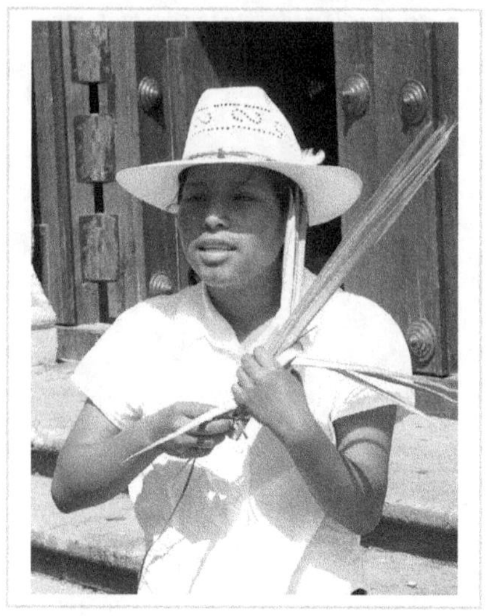

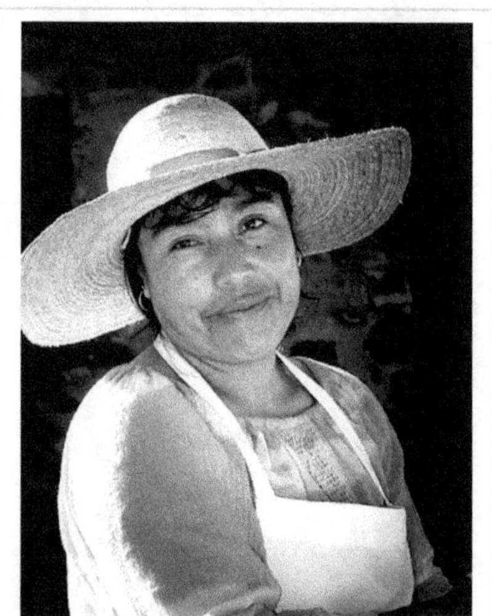

In the top photo, the photographer did not use fill flash and as a result the face is not fully illuminated.
In the bottom photo, with the use of the on-camera flash as fill-flash, the photographer illuminated the shadowed part of the subject's face under the hat along with the subject's eyes.

In 1852, Englishman Rev. George Bridges became one of the earliest travel photographers when he visited Egypt and the Mediterranean using paper negatives to document the landscape.

Chapter Eight, Find The Editors

Once you have some potentially marketable photos you must find and approach editors who will buy those photos.

You might already have a print magazine or a web magazine in mind, if so, you can find the editor's contact information on the masthead of that magazine located within the first few pages or at the bottom of the web page.

Web Search

If you have no target magazine you can find listings of magazines and editors on the web. There you can find stock agencies, stock portals, trade magazines, web magazines, and travel magazines. Once you find a magazine's home page you will find links to the editor's name, contact info, and to the photographer's guidelines.

Photographer's Market

A good source of editor information will be the publication by Northlight Books, *The Photographer's Market*. This annually published book is available in web and print versions ($20-$25 USD Amazon) (kindle $17 USD) where it lists editors and publications that buy the rights to the use of photos.

A similar publication, *The Writer's Market*, from Writers Digest Books contains over 2,000 names and addresses of magazine editors, book publishers, and editors of publications that review photo and text packages. *www.writersmarket.com/*

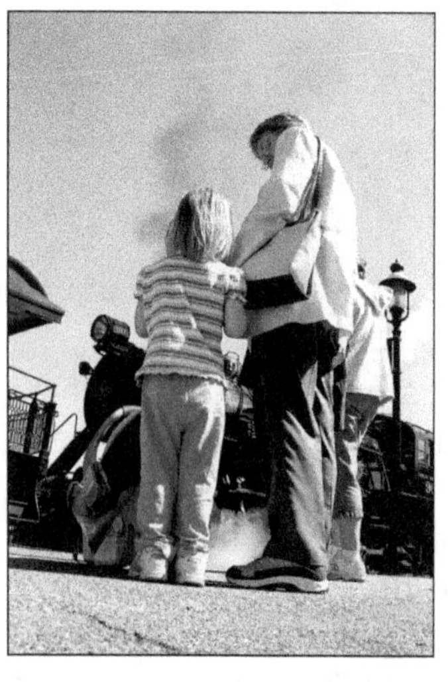

Include people and vary the point of view. In this case shooting low to give a child's view of a train ride

Articles within these websites and books give details on how to approach editors and how to get your photos and text reviewed.

First, of course, you must identify your chosen market and tailor your work for that market.

What are those markets?

Markets For Your Photos

For the photographer starting out, three areas most open to you will be the stock agency or web stock portal, the newspaper or web magazine that publishes photo features, or the web magazine, print magazine, or newspaper where the photos become part of a feature article and you supply photos while you or a collaborator write the text.

Stock Agency, Photo Feature, or Article

Although opportunities to sell your photos are many and varied, these three common avenues are most open to the beginning digital photographer who would like to sell travel photos.

- ***The Stock Agency:*** An agency acts as your sales representative, they will place your photos with editors for one-time use while they take a 40%-60% commission from the proceeds.
- ***The Photo Feature:*** You create a carefully-captioned and contiguous theme photo essay that you deliver to a print magazine, web magazine, or newspaper.
- ***The Text and Photo Feature:*** You combine your photos with a 400 to 1,200 word article that you or a collaborator write and that you illustrate with your captioned photos.

Each of these approaches to selling the use of your photos starts in the same way and that is with a letter of proposal or query letter.

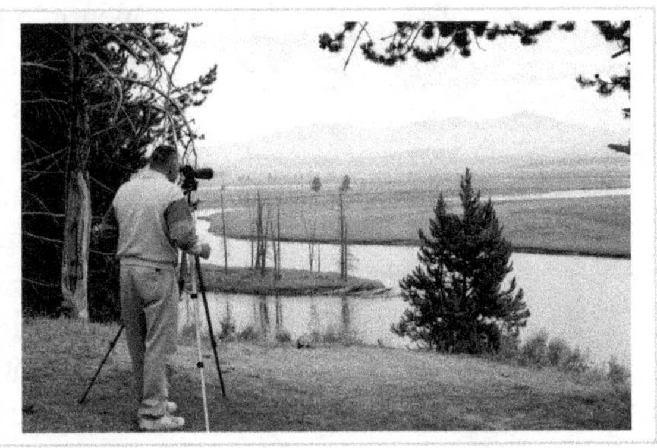

Vacation places can bring photos of people enjoying nature and can give the reader the feeling that they too can enjoy what you did, watching eagles and wolves on the Yellowstone River.

The Markets

The following is an in-depth look at each of the markets most open to beginning freelance photographers.

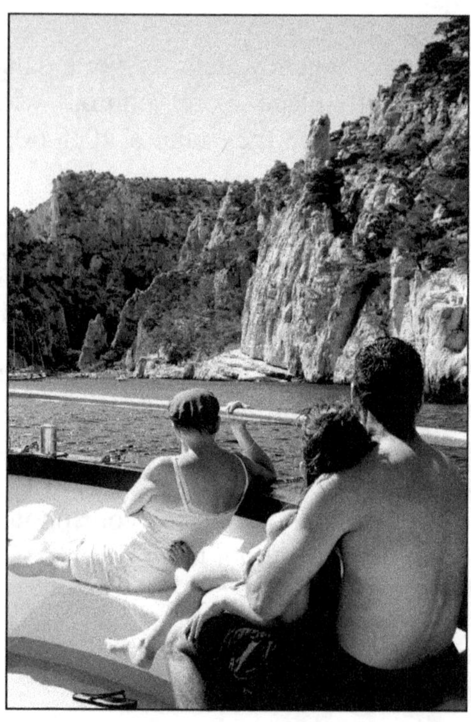

Include people in your travel photos. By backing a bit here you include the cliffs on the Mediterranean while also creating the sense of vacationers involved in sightseeing

Stock Agency

A stock agency acts as your sales agent and advertises your photos for inclusion in textbooks, magazines, advertising brochures, and dozens of other applications. The price they ask will depend on the size of the photo that appears in the publication and the publication's circulation.

A typical sale of rights that you grant may be that the publication can reprint your photo at a quarter of a page in a school textbook and will use the photo for five years.

This could bring you $100 USD after the agency's commission. Other factors will determine price; the agency will broker the agreement.

Proceeds

The stock agency splits the proceeds with you, usually taking 40% and higher of the income generated. They do not sell the image; they license or grant the rights to use the image for a specified time and in a specified media. The agency handles the details of the sale of rights based on your preference.

Selling or Renting

When placing your photos for publication, you or the agency will be licensing the use of the photo for a specific publication and for a specific length of time. You will not actually sell the photo; it is more like renting.

You will always retain the right to the photo and can license the use many times into the future.

Restrictions

You can impose restrictions on the use of your images based on your desire to keep your photos from appearing in publications that advocate causes or life styles not to your liking. You always retain rights to your images and you can ask for them back or withdraw them from the market at any time. Some agencies, however, will have a withdrawal fee. Their contract will address this.

Patience

With steady work and patience you could have success with agencies but it is best to find a seldom-photographed niche and be prepared to work at it for the long haul. Agencies recommend that you stay at it for at least five years and that you send them a steady supply of up-to-date photos. You can send photos to several agencies.

Although this is a very competitive arena, your study and understanding of this avenue to sales can greatly upgrade your knowledge of the marketability of a photograph and your ability to deliver photographs that meet a photo editor's needs. The financial rewards may be slow in coming, unless you have a special niche, but the lessons learned will be invaluable and you can apply those lessons to other markets.

After buyers begin to notice your work, sales could increase dramatically. Patience and persistence will be the keys to success in stock agency sales.

Web Portal

The web has virtual stock agencies of sorts called portals that represent members. Some have membership fees of up to $500 while others take only a commission. They circulate thumbnails of your photos on the web and sell one-time use of the image from photos that you send as jpegs via the internet or from a CD or other media that you send them. The agency then sends copies of the photo directly to the client via the internet.

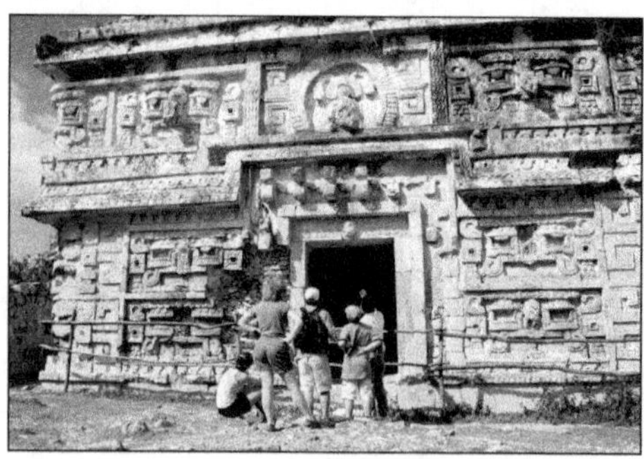

People give a photo scale and additional interest. Many editors want 95 % of the travel photos that they publish to have people in them.

Starting Out

One good agency for a freelance photographer starting out would be the web-based portal called Alamy, a Great Britain based company that will take a 40% - 60% commission on sales but has no up-front cost to the photographer. They have a nimble web search system that makes it easy for buyers to find a specific image quickly. Their clients include in-flight magazines and other upscale publications as well as textbook publishers and many others.

Research

Before you decide on an agency, conduct your own search of stock photography websites from a buyer's perspective and see how quickly you can find a certain niche or category. If you can find your niche very quickly at an agency's website and it is not flooded with images, this agency could be a good target for your images.

Low Cost

You can keep your costs low, other than the time spent preparing the submission that you send to the agency, and you can still use your images elsewhere, in most cases, while copies of them reside on the portal's web site where they are available to buyers.

We have not mentioned so called Micro Stock agencies because the pay-outs are tiny (micro) but these agencies might be of interest to you in starting out.

Exclusive

There are agencies that will want exclusive us of your photos, that is, they will be the only agency that will represent and market particular photos of yours.

This might be a niche agency that could be beneficial to you if the agency is selling widely because the agency will get the best price for the use of your photos since they can control the distribution and offer the buyer exclusive use.

On the other hand, if the agency is not selling widely and regularly, this could tie up your valuable images.
You should therefore research the agency before signing an exclusive contract and be mindful of withdrawal fees.

We look next at the other avenues open to beginning freelance photographers, the web magazines, trade papers, and newspapers.

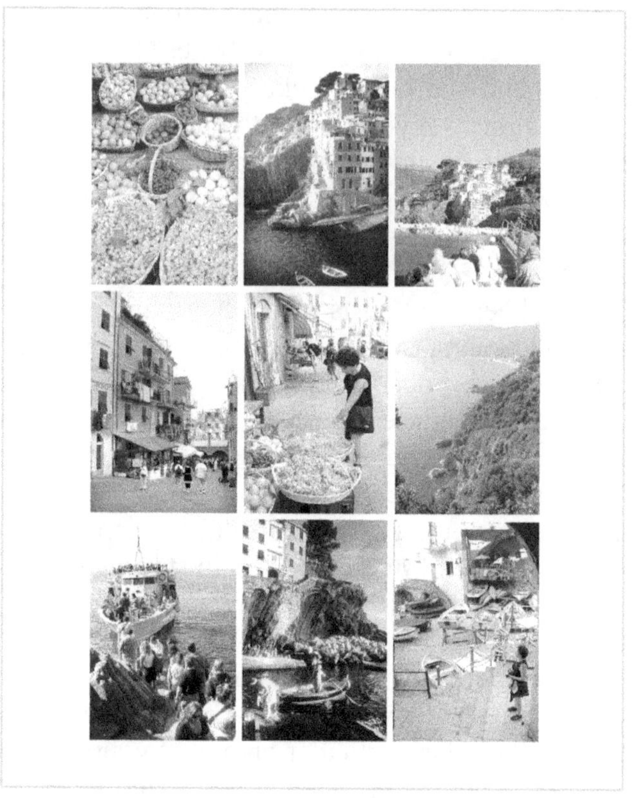

A sample of photos available for a photo feature about Cinque Terre, Italy

The Magazine and Newspaper Photo Feature

Check in the *Photographer's Market* (available in your public library, bookstores, and on the web) for editors who list their interest in reviewing photos for a photo feature. This would be a carefully-captioned group of photos with a contiguous theme that tells a story.

You approach the editor in the same way, with a query letter (email or paper) and a sample sheet or two of your photos. Email or paper mail both and explain what your feature will be about, what ISO you used, film or digital, the format used: medium, large, or 35 mm, and when you can deliver the captioned photos. Include your contact information, email, and if you are submitting by traditional letter, a self-addressed, stamped envelope.

Once you make the sale, deliver the photos with meticulous captioning according to the editor's request.

Next we look at the *Feature Article*

Text and Photo Articles

Another way for a freelancer to sell photos is to combine 400 to 1,200 words of text with captioned photos and sell it to the web magazine, print magazine, or newspaper market.

Propose an idea or a travel destination feature through a one-page query letter and a sample page or two of the images that you have available to support the article.

Write the article or collaborate with a writer and support the text with carefully captioned photos.

A collaborative effort by artist and writer is attractive to editors because they can simplify their acquisition process by dealing with one person or a team.

Trade Papers

Trade papers are a neglected source of sales for photographers because they are not glamorous. They can be a great source of sales, however, and by searching the web you can find thousands of trade magazines and trade newspapers that are often a good and overlooked source of sales.

See ***www.mondotimes.com*** for a list of over 18,000 trade publications, many that work with freelance photographers and writers.

Caption Reminder

Forgive the second reminder on this one but remember that regardless of which market you approach, trade, travel, or stock, you must take good notes while you photograph. Pay particular attention to the spelling of proper names of people, streets, towns, and cities. Each of these avenues of sales for you will depend not only on good sound photos but on carefully captioned photos. Accurate captions become part of your reputation.

As someone who started out being sloppy about documenting I can tell you that you will resent every minute of going online to check spelling and every dollar you spend calling a source to verify information.

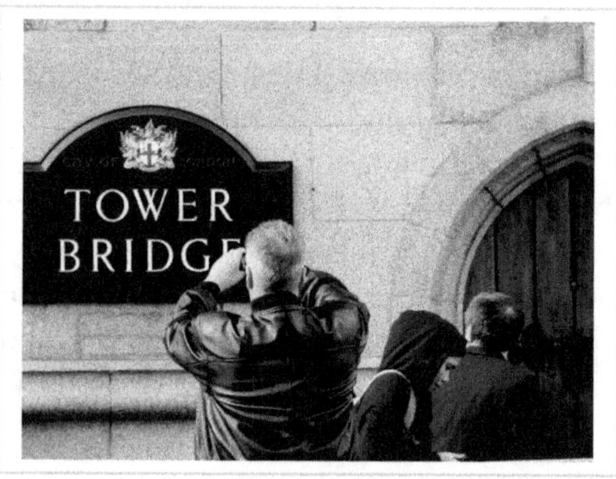

Make photos of signs in distant places if that is what it takes to get the spelling correct. It may not be possible to return. This one may seem obvious but many visitors mistakenly call the Tower Bridge in London, "London Bridge."

Other Markets

The previously mentioned book the, "Photographer's Market," lists many other markets open to beginning photographers such as trade and industry newspapers, calendars, postcards, and greeting card companies.

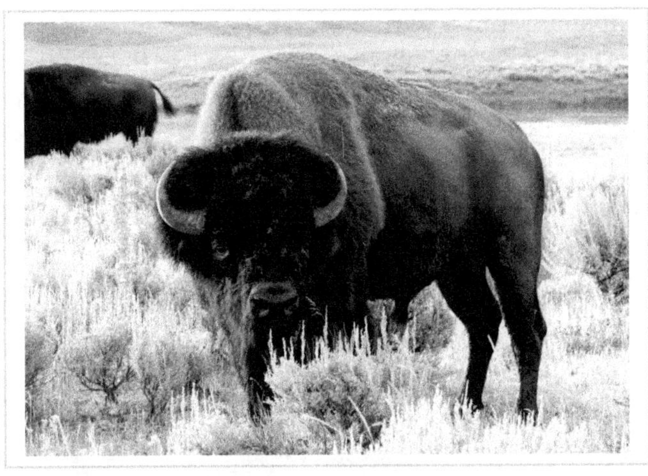

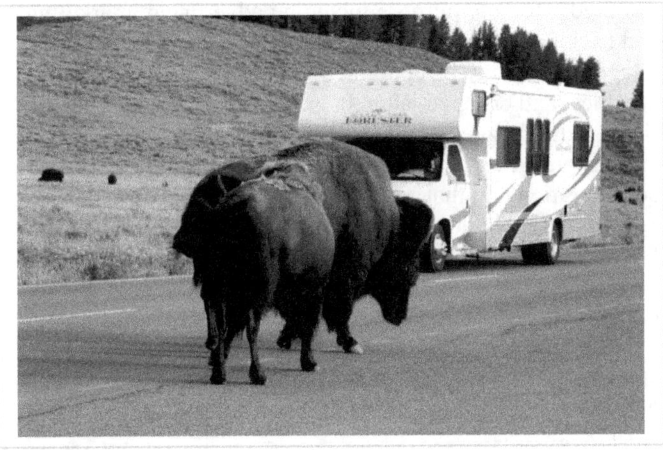

An animal alone might be a good subject for a nature article but for a travel article it may be more interesting and appropriate to show animals interacting with people.

Sample Model Release

When you are investigating markets for your photos you will often see that the photo editor or agency requests a model release. Stock photo agencies, particularly, will want any photo of people, recognizable or not, to be accompanied by a written release, a signed document giving the photographer permission to use the photo.

Stock agencies target a wider market than magazines and if you therefore couple your photos sent to an agency with a written release your photos will have more value. They will have commercial potential (in advertising) as well as value in editorial use. (travel articles and such)

Sample Model Release

Photographic Model Release

For consideration received, I__________*Model'sName*_______
give______________*Photographer's Name*___________________
and assigns my permission to license the images of me in any media for any purpose including advertising, marketing and packaging for any product or service. I agree that the images of me may be combined with other images, text and graphics, and cropped, altered, or modified. I agree that all rights to the images of me belong to ____*Photographer*______ and assigns. I agree that I have no further right to additional consideration and that I will make no further claim.
I agree that this release is binding upon my heirs and assigns.
I agree that this release is irrevocable worldwide.
I am at least 18 years of age and have the full legal capacity to give this permission.

Signature____________*Model Name*____________________
Address____
City _________________________________ State ________
Country ________________________ Zip Code_____________
Phone _______________________ Email____________________

You can print this short-form release on a card with your inkjet printer and carry it in your camera bag. *See detailed release on page 93.*

Model Release

In valuable consideration of my engagement as a mode, I _______*Model*_________ upon the terms herewith stated, give to ____________*Photographer*_____________ his/her heirs, legal representatives and assigns, those for whom the Photographer is acting, and those acting with his or her authority and permission:

A. The unrestricted right and permission forever to copyright and use, re-use, publish, and republish photographic portraits or pictures of me or in which I may be included intact or in part, composite or distorted in character or form, without restriction as to changes or transformations in conjunction with my own or a fictitious name, or reproduction hereof in color or otherwise, made through any and all media now or hereafter known for illustration, art, promotion, advertising, trade, or any other purpose whatsoever.

B. I also permit the use of any text material in connection therewith.

C. I hereby relinquish any right that I may have to examine or approve the completed product or products or the advertising copy or printed matter that may be used in conjunction therewith or the use to which it may be applied.

D. I hereby release, discharge and agree to save harmless the Photographer, his/her heirs, legal representatives or assigns, and all persons functioning under his/her permission or authority or those for whom he/she is functioning, from any liability by virtue of any blurring, distortion, alteration, optical illusion, or use in composite form whether intentional or otherwise, that may occur or be produced in the taking of said picture or in any subsequent processing thereof, as well as any publication thereof, including without limitation any claims for libel or invasion of privacy.

E. I hereby affirm that I am over the age of 18 and have the right to contract in my own name. I have read the above authorization, release and agreement, prior to its execution; I fully understand the contents thereof. This agreement shall be binding upon me and my heirs, legal representatives and assigns.
I am also aware that these terms are subject to negotiation, deletion or addendum, which may be valid if handwritten on this release and initialed and dated by both parties, the photographer and me next to the modification or any modification that is typed and signed by both parties.
Modifications may be implied by any releases/contracts with my employer (Professional Models)without my notice by the Photographer.

Address of Model____
Phone number ______________________and e-mail_____________________

Date Signed: ____/____/____

Name of Model _____________________Signature of Model_________________

Signature of Witness____

You will read that you do not need a model release for a photo that a publication will use in an editorial format, that is, one used to illustrate an article or a newsworthy event. And while it is true that a photo used in an application other than to sell a product does not need a release, many editors, including those of travel magazines prefer to receive released photos regardless of how they will use the photo.

Niche

When searching the Writer's and Photographer's Market books, pay close attention to what each editor wants. Their needs are detailed in the guidelines and if you follow those guidelines closely you will get results. Choose to send your material to editors who closely match your niche. Use the books to identify your niche if you don't already have one. (what do you really love to photograph?) Once you find a niche, specialize in that field until you are the local expert and then go on to become the national expert. (could be as photographer, travel expert, wine expert, food expert, adventurer, bike traveler, hiker, snowboarder, skateboarder, fly fisherman, grafitero, etc but it must be something that you love.) Find the editors in that niche and target them with your query letters and photo samples.

Although the internet and the economy have diminished the print magazine market there are still over a thousand print magazines in English-speaking countries that can be paying markets for your work.

Query

Proposals to the editors of all of these markets start with a query letter. In the next chapter we look more closely at the query letter and how to craft a professional proposal

Two early US travel photographers, Timothy O'Sullivan and William Henry Jackson, used the collodion wet plate process in the 1870s to make landscapes in the relatively unsettled west, Jackson in Yellowstone, O'Sullivan in the Grand Canyon.

Chapter Nine, The Query Letter

Although email queries are the preferred method of contact for many editors, the #10 business envelope still has its value as a query letter. It all depends on what type of query the editor will accept.

This short business letter, email or paper letter, could be all that stands between you and getting your travel photos published. It is as simple as telling the editor what you have and getting lucky enough or being prepared enough that the editor has a need at that moment for your material. Competition is stiff, your query letter is your showcase and you must make it strong and appropriate.

Simplicity

Check the photographers/writers guidelines from the publication to determine which method of contact the editor prefers, email or traditional paper letter.

Simplicity and research are the keys. The editor or an assistant will look at many letters or emails each day and they will give little time to long or inappropriate letters.

Study the magazine and then make the first paragraph of your letter tell the story in that magazine's language, make your sample images do their own talking, Tell the editor about any language skills, photo processing skills and any audio video work you have done. Then provide clear contact information in a professional manner and limit it to one page. In short, make it easy for the editor to work with you.

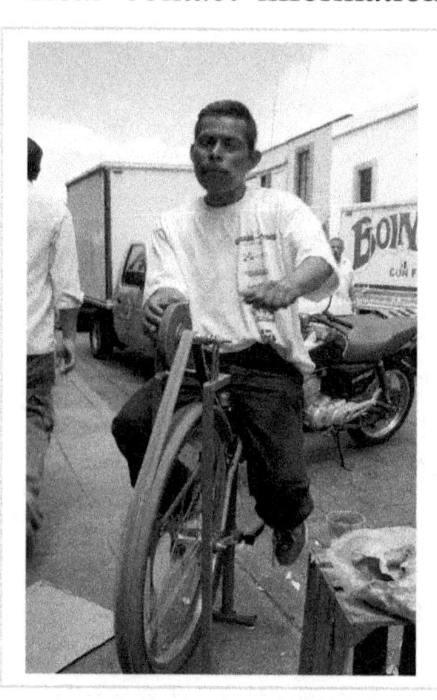

Street scenes in countries foreign to you can add interest to a photo feature but model releases of street people could be tough to get and at times impossible unless you will be visiting long enough to gain the trust of the subject. Editors of travel magazines, however, will use unreleased photos at times in an editorial context.

Use good stationery if you are mailing queries but not expensive stationery, you will mail many proposals, possibly as many as ten letters for each assignment that you receive when you are starting out.

Use a good printer when using paper mail. Print with black ink and a readable type style such as Times New Roman at font size 12.

Keep it simple, direct, clean, and limit your query letter to 300-400 words-one page. Most important, don't fear rejection; try to learn from it.

Query Without Clips

In the following sample query letter offering a text and photo package, the photographer mentions no previous publications, the best practice when you are starting out and you have no clips. (samples of published work) Better to say nothing than to make an excuse.

Sample Query Letter

Julie Augustin, Editor
Sports X Magazine
906 N. Michigan Rd.
San Carmel, IL. 04352

Date:
Dear Ms. Augustin:

Moab, Utah attracts outdoor adventurers from the world over. They come to Moab bringing high-tech sports toys to test their mettle on Moab's towering red rock, the austere desert, and the unpredictable Colorado River.
Each year in September we hike and mountain bike on the many Moab trails and canoe and kayak the Colorado. While there we make photos of this tortured landscape, a high desert that offers ultimate freedom while at the same time demanding respect.
From the Slick Rock Bike trail to the Arches above the Colorado River, Moab is a rough-chiseled work-in-progress responding to the elemental forces of nature. Wind and water still shape its rocks, high, red, and interesting enough to entice climbers, hikers, four-wheelers, and campers to come and enjoy the rocky playground.
To make it even better, the Colorado River runs through town and offers rafters, jet boaters, and kayakers a thrill of a lifetime.
I would like to send you an article of 1200 words about Moab Utah and the extreme and not so extreme outdoor sport available to visitors.
I can supply digital photos as 13x19 inch, 60 meg TIFF files on CD or as you request.
I have captions for all photos and recognizable people have signed releases. I will include a list of accommodations and sport renters and local maps to accompany the article.
I have enclosed a sample of photos available. I can deliver text and photos at your request.

Thanks, Sincerely,

Passive Language

Use active verbs in your query letter instead of the passive verb. Rather than say, "The images can be delivered," say, "I will deliver the images." Rather than say, "The photos were taken," say, "I took the photos." Rather than say, "The photos are released," say, "I have releases for the photos."

This small change in the way you write your letter could make a big difference in the way the editor views your ability to take responsibility and to deliver what you have proposed. Your use of active language can make a big difference in your ability to write strong captions and to write a feature article if you choose to try that route to selling photos.

You can activate the passive language checker in the spell and grammar check options in the word processing program that you use. Active verbs will help you sell your product and sell yourself.

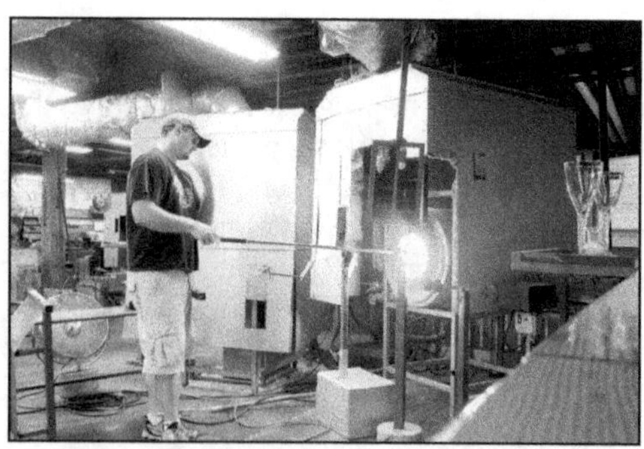

Send both verticals and horizontals in your samples; editors often lament the shortage of verticals (Portrait mode). By sending verticals and horizontal (such as photo above) you give the editor options.

Email Query Letter With Samples

Email is the least expensive tool for you to reach the editors with your proposal and samples. In that email put a one-page business letter (250-300 words) that tells the editor who you are and what you would like to send them.

With the letter you send a sample of your work. The sample could be an attached page or two of photos, a jpeg file of 8x12 inches, 300 pixels per inch resulting in a 4 to 8 megabyte file, 9 images per page, that demonstrate the quality of your work and its theme. (Make it 300 ppi so that the editor can zoom in to check sharpness)

Include with your letter and samples your email and contact information. This is the showcase of your work and it should be your best effort.

If you are sending a query by traditional mail include a self-addressed stamped envelope for the editor's reply.

The email or paper letter will include your name, address, telephone number, and email address along with information about the type of material that you have: digital, slide, negative, or print, and how you will deliver that material.

Include reproductions of clips (magazine pages of your published photos or articles) of previous publications if you have them.

When the query goes to the editor in an email, along with your attached photos, keep in mind that many editors will not open emails with attachments because of the virus threat. Therefore your sample photos could go as an attachment in a follow-up email.

Send a traditional letter query with printed samples if the editor will review letters. Your photos to support your idea, printed in color on Epson double-sided matte paper, (no bleed through) with verticals on one side and horizontals on the other to save paper and postage, will be your showcase. This sample can go into the envelope with the query letter.

The benefit of the paper submission is that the page of photos may circulate to other editors within the same organization.

Once you make contact with an editor or once you successfully submit photos for publication your correspondence will be primarily by email.

Website

Another showcase for your work will be to maintain a website with samples of your images for the editors review. You must do this well to show your photos at their best. Use large photos in the website and show your photos quickly, without flash, passwords, "Enter Here," pages or other sorts of web gadgetry that will come between the editor and a quick look at your photos.

Allow for manual clicking of slide shows so that an editor can easily go forward or back.

Research the subject of your sample photos and give each photo a lucid caption that demonstrates your attention to detail. Keep your presentation in the realm of journalism. You can still be artistic without being cute or artsy.

Use simple navigation on your website and include precise contact information.

Free Web Hosting

You can find hosting for free with limited page counts. Free hosting sites will offer five or ten pages, all you need to demonstrate photos and you need only pay for the domain name, about $15-$20 dollars annually.

Multiple Query Letters

Circulate more than one proposal at a time by paper submission or email but do not offer the same images to editors of competing magazines at the same time.

Query Letter Sample

John Jones
PO Box 53
North Adams, MA 03091
1-617-334-4981
info@jjones.com
Date________

Mary Goult, Editor
New England Shopping Vacations
25 Yardarm Drive
Dennisport, MA 83701

Dear Ms. Goult:

From the Gilded Age mansions of Newport, Rhode Island to the historic whaling village of Fair Haven, galleries on The Coastal Villages Trail hold many 17th century masterpieces of stone, bone, ceramic, and wood once prized by New England sea captains. While gallery hopping on these coastal roads we photographed an antique shop owner, an up-scale art gallery owner, a farm stand proprietor selling fresh produce and flowers, a vineyard owner, and the manager of a bakery ranked top ten in the country.

The interviews will go into extended captions accompanying sense-of-place, released photos of these folks in the villages on the coast of Rhode Island Sound, a place where you feel like you have stepped back to 17th century and life in the age of sail.
I would like to propose a photo feature for your "Weekend Escape" section about the seaside life of the New England mariners and their homes on Rhode Island's Coastal Village Trail. We will feature the modern people who now live in these homes and run the galleries along the coast.
I photographed digitally at 100- ISO and have photos that are available as 13 x 19 inch 300 dpi TIFF files.
The photos are available on CD as tiff files or sent via modem as jpegs as you direct along with the captions in MS Word and the releases in word. I can deliver this material for your review immediately. I have enclosed a sample of some of the images available for this photo feature.

Sincerely,

John Jones
info@Jonesphoto.com

Photo Sample

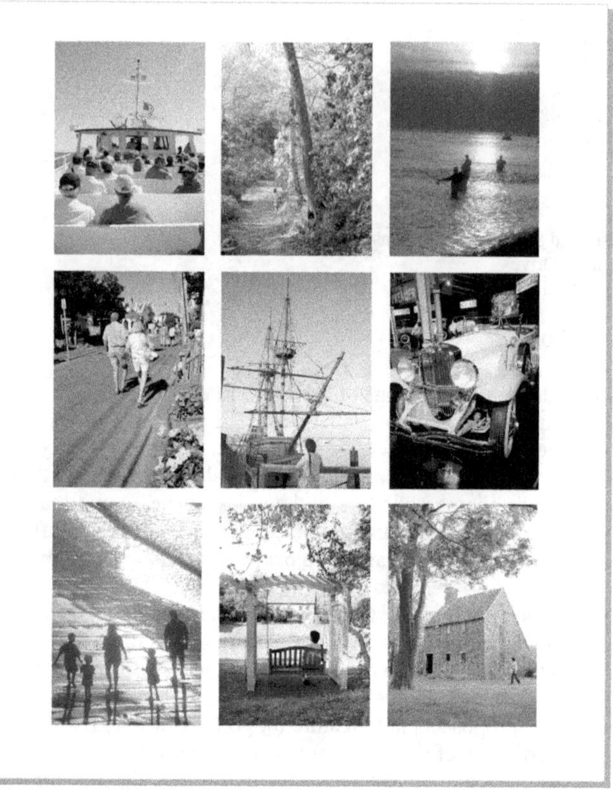

A photo sample such as the one above, showing your work tightly linked to your proposal, will accompany your query letter. The sample is a good introduction of your work to a photo editor. This could be an email attachment, a jpeg file of 8x12 inches, 300 pixels per inch resulting in an 8 megabyte file of nine photos that demonstrate the quality of your work and its theme.

You can do the same with a paper print.
The value of a paper sample over an email attachment is that the sample could circulate to other editors within a publishing house that produces several magazines.

Photographer's Guidelines, Editorial Calendar

Give yourself a head start; write to several magazines and request their photographer's guidelines and their editorial calendar.

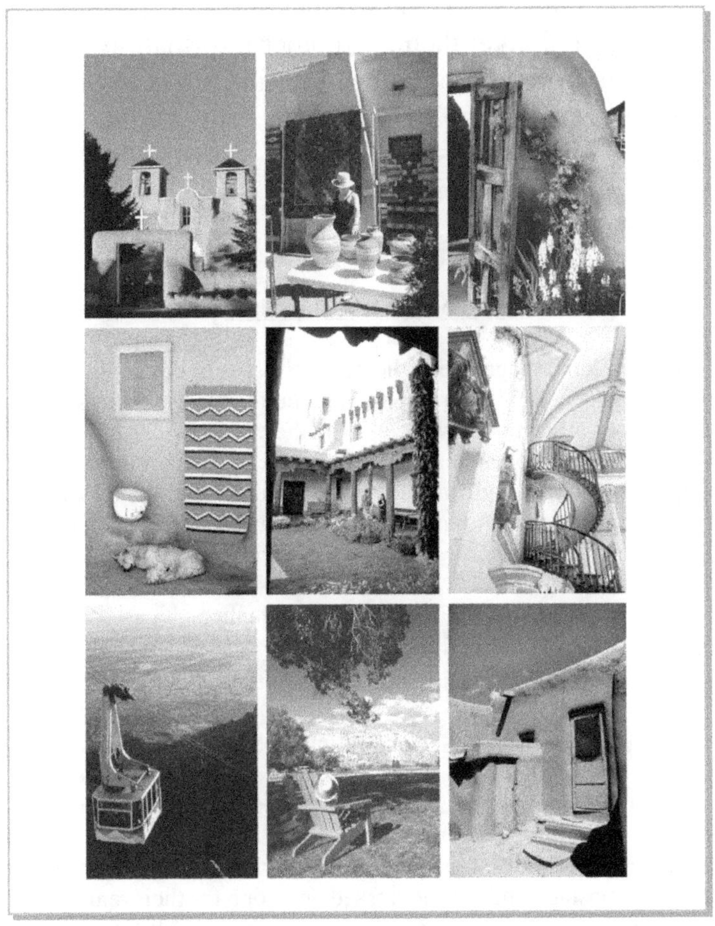

This sample of photos would accompany a proposal for a Santa Fe/Taos-theme photo feature.

While few magazines share their editorial calendar, some will send a list of areas that the publication will cover during the upcoming year.

The Photographer's Guidelines

The photographer's guidelines describe the style of photos that the magazine will review, the method you should use to deliver them, and other information that will help you to offer appropriate photos in your query letter.

Guidelines and the calendar can help you understand what the editor wants and deliver just what the editor needs at just the right time.

> Photographer's Guidelines
>
> Our national magazine dedicates each issue to covering people, sports, politics, art, literature, and the high-tech toys of the outdoor adventurer. We welcome the contributions of creative photographers that can capture the essence of our magazine and although we use photos from photographers known to us and we use stock photography, we have sections open to freelance photographers. Study the magazine before submitting.
>
> Open to Freelance Photographers:
>
> - Photo Feature, front of the book
> - Our gallery section devoted to outdoor photography and photographers
> - The Back of the Book section, open to freelance photographers
>
> Send digital images on CD accompanied by a printed contact sheet of thumbnails.
>
> Send duplicate slides, transparencies, or prints for review with adequate postage and self-addressed envelope for their return at our request. Do not send original material unless fulfilling an assignment.
>
> We cannot be responsible for unsolicited material.

Photographers Guidelines

Thank you for your interest in contributing to our Magazine. We publish ten issues a year. Our intent is to illustrate new and fresh destinations for travelers. Our Travel articles capture the sense of the place, its sights, and sounds and smells just the way the traveler can find them. We want to inspire readers to go to that place just as the photographer did.

Read several copies of our magazine and you will see that we cover the U.S. and many foreign countries and that we are interested in places that the average traveler can visit. We feature adventure travel, mainstream travel, and independent travel, but always with a concern for the environment.

Our photo features cover a small area in depth; we do not do broad overviews of locations. Tightly focus your view of an area and cover its history, culture, museums, ruins, national parks, nature preserves, cuisine, regional dance, and festival. Tell a story with your photos and captions.

We always look for the fresh idea and accept freelance query letters for all sections of the magazine.

Our postcards section is always open to unpublished freelancers and is a good place to break in with us. We do accept queries from unpublished photographers that have studied our magazine.

Clips

Include clips if you have created recently published work while on assignment.

Query

Query by letter only and include clips and samples. Focus the query to one location; we do not consider general or vague queries.

Keep your query focused to one well-developed proposal that you have created specifically for our magazine and that has a strong or unique slant. A successful query will have a strong topic sentence or two that tells the story and a body that tells us that you are the person to deliver the photos on this story. Tell us why this story is important, why you are the one to photograph it, and why it is right for our magazine.

Continued on next page

Accompany proposals with a page or two of sample thumbnails of supporting photos. We will consider all proposals, but we receive many and must reject a good percentage even when they meet all the requirements.

If we accept your proposal and assign the piece, we will describe the terms clearly in a written contract. We buy First North American Serial Rights

Photo Requirements:

Include people in your photographs. They should be enjoying travel activities that are available in the place you are covering. Show wide angle, close-ups, twilight, street scenes, restaurants, museums, ruins, and other tourist attractions. We like to give the reader a sense of the place. We only publish photos of activities that are approved by local authority and that are friendly to the environment.

Captions

Create caption information that tells the: who, what, when, where why and how of the place.

Include in your captions, where possible, quotes from people you have photographed. Secure written permission to use those photographs from the subject along with the subject's telephone number or email address.

Digital photos reproduce better if they are slightly overexposed rather than underexposed. The use of fill flash and balanced exposure will enhance the ability of the printer to reproduce the photo.

We consider color slide, transparency, and unsharpened digital material only, except in the case of historical photographs that enhance the story. We do not accept sandwiched digital photos.

Send proposals to:

Photo Editor

Sample Magazine

Study sample magazines. If not available in local stores write and request sample magazines to help you identify each publication's photo style further and to give you concrete direction in making photos for publication. Once you have sample magazines and their photo guidelines, you can tailor your photo style and content to your target magazine or newspaper.

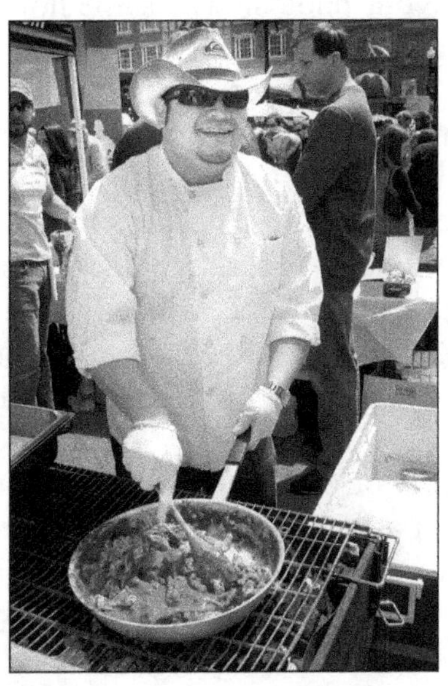

Cover restaurants and celebrity chefs if possible; travelers love to dine on the regional cuisine.

The Readership

Keep in mind that the products offered by a magazine in its advertisements reflect the economic status of the readership and are your cue to styling your photos; know the readers of the magazine, their economic status, what they wear, and where they like to go for entertainment and recreation. Some magazines will send a demographic breakdown of the readership in their photographer/writers guidelines.

Query With Appropriate Sample

Once you have studied the guides and the sample magazine you can write better focused query letters and you will send more appropriate samples of your photos with your query letter.

Offer Variety In Sample Photos

Offer as many vertical photos as horizontals. (portrait mode and landscape mode) Tightly restrict the photos to a theme. This will let the photo editor know that you can supply photos for a photo feature and that you will offer choices in laying out a feature.

Never send a CD of digital images, just your attached sample photos that give a quick look at your work.

Send large file photos only when you have made the sale and the editor has asked for your photos. The same holds true for original slides or transparency material. Send no photo material (digital or paper) unless you have an assignment and the magazine wants your photos for inclusion in a publication.

If the editor wants to review photos, be sure to send copies and keep your originals. This is much less expensive with digital equipment than it is with film. The photos go via a CD or attached to an email and you always keep copies of your original digital files and your archived raw files.

When you propose a theme or offer your photos to an editor, create your samples in a file of 9 images per page. For paper samples print them on ink jet, matte paper such as Epson Double-Sided Matte. These samples will show that you can offer editors choices in designing an article.

Put your contact info, email on the bottom of each printed sample page.

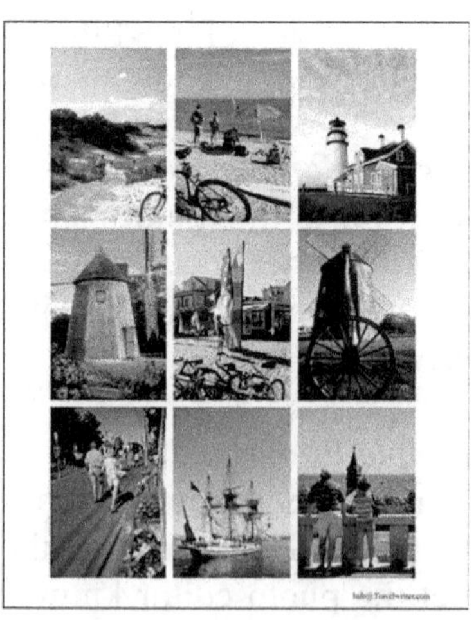

Nine photos on an 8.5 x 11 page of inkjet matte paper printed in color will tell the editor what photos you have to support a photo feature or a magazine article.

Photographer's Guidelines

If you would like to contribute photography to our magazine, please study recent issues and study our photographic style. We prefer color transparencies but also consider digital material. We also consider 5x7 or larger B&W or color prints on glossy paper. We do not accept negatives,

Your name and address should accompany each submission or slide, accompanied by a cover letter with details of the submission and good contact information.
Return should include a street address for FedEx or other carrier that you specify.
Returns of your photo material can take up to 4 months unless you request an expedited return. (You must cover the shipping costs for their return)

We pay for the use of your photos upon publication in a varying scale that depends on the photo size, the type, and how large we use the photo.
We encourage submissions of current events. Once we use your photos, we will include you on a mailing list of our contributors and you will receive a calendar of our upcoming photo needs.

Photos we look for usually fall into one of the following categories:
Cover: We prefer color vertical photos related to a feature story.
See back issues of our magazine and study the placement of text as a guide for composing a cover photo.
Photo Feature: Color slides or large digital files of a themed topic.
Ideas for the photo feature considered via query letter or fax.
End of Book photo: transparency or large digital file
Digital Photo Guidelines:
Digital photos: Half page or less: 6 inches by 8 inches at 300 dpi
Full page or double page: 11 by 16 inches at 300 dpi
Photos must be accompanied by a corresponding, numbered, contact sheet, keyed to the caption information.
Otherwise, send a digital file folder containing 72 dpi thumbnails of your photos with labels keyed to the captions.

Send files only in Photoshop TIFF, or Photoshop compressed JPEG
We prefer digital photos sent via CD
Send to Photo Editor

Creating The Samples

Imaging software makes the creation of these samples pages to show your work relatively straightforward once you learn the image management tools.

One way is set up a 3x3 photo sheet at 300 dpi. (nine photos arranged three across and three down) with each photo neatly presented. Don't show the captions or file numbers, just the photos as neatly arranged as possible. For jpeg attachments, flatten the image if it is in layers and size it as a jpeg for sending via email. (Eight inches by twelve inches by 300 PPI)

For print samples this same file, 8.5 x 11 inch, can be printed in color at a high printer resolution. The printed samples will go along with a printed query letter and you will include a self-addressed stamped envelope for the editor's reply.

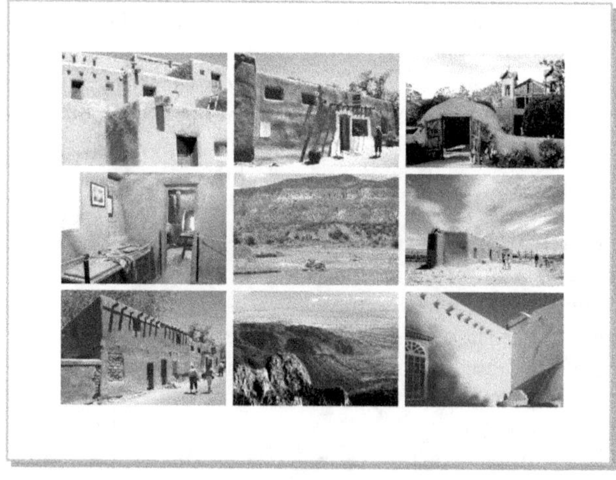

A sample page of horizontal photos and a page of vertical photos will show that you are able to use variety in your photography and that you can offer a photo editor flexibility in the layout of the magazine. A file eight inches by eleven inches by 300 PPI will result in a 6-megabyte file that can be attached to an email

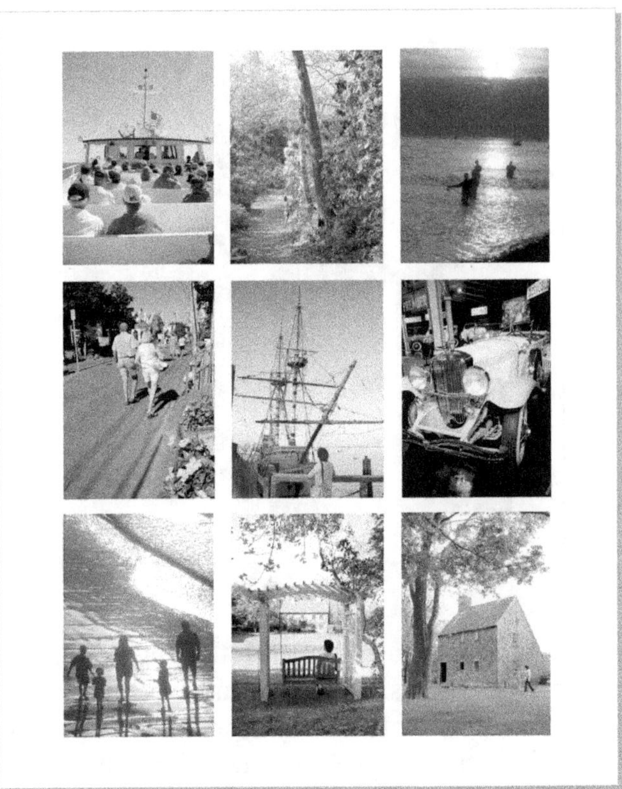

You need not worry about getting the paper samples back as they are inexpensive enough to make. You are best to leave them with the editor along with your business card and contact info. You hope that the editor saves them for reference and possible future assignment or passes them on to other editors.

Put your email address on the bottom of each sample because the sample may circulate to other editors and they will need contact information. Many magazines have several divisions and a host of publications working from the same offices.

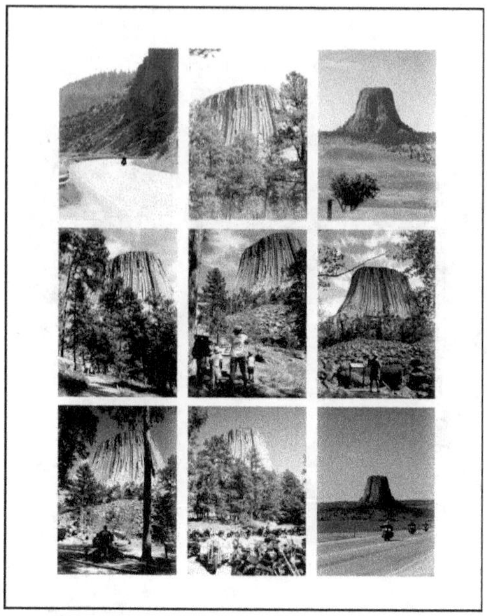

You might receive a rejection letter regarding a photo feature proposal but six months later be asked by the editor to cover an event or a location. It might even be a different editor that will email you and ask that you take on the assignment that originally received the rejection. Your sample photos sold the editor on your ability to deliver good photo work in a professional manner. Let your quality samples do your talking, you will have no better showcase.

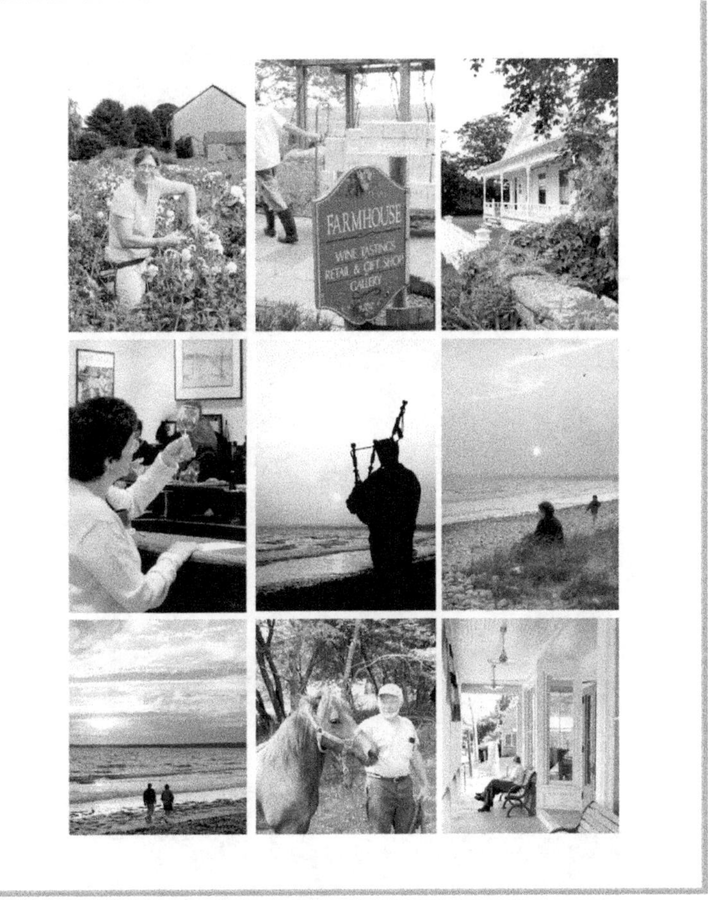

A sample of nine photos per page should adequately show your work.

This sample of photos printed on inkjet paper at nine photos per page will accompany your query letter. Nine verticals on one side, nine horizontals on the other side.

This same file, 8.5 inches by 11 inches at 300 ppi at 6 megabytes can be attached to an email query letter, one digital file of verticals, (portrait mode) one of horizontal images. (landscape mode)

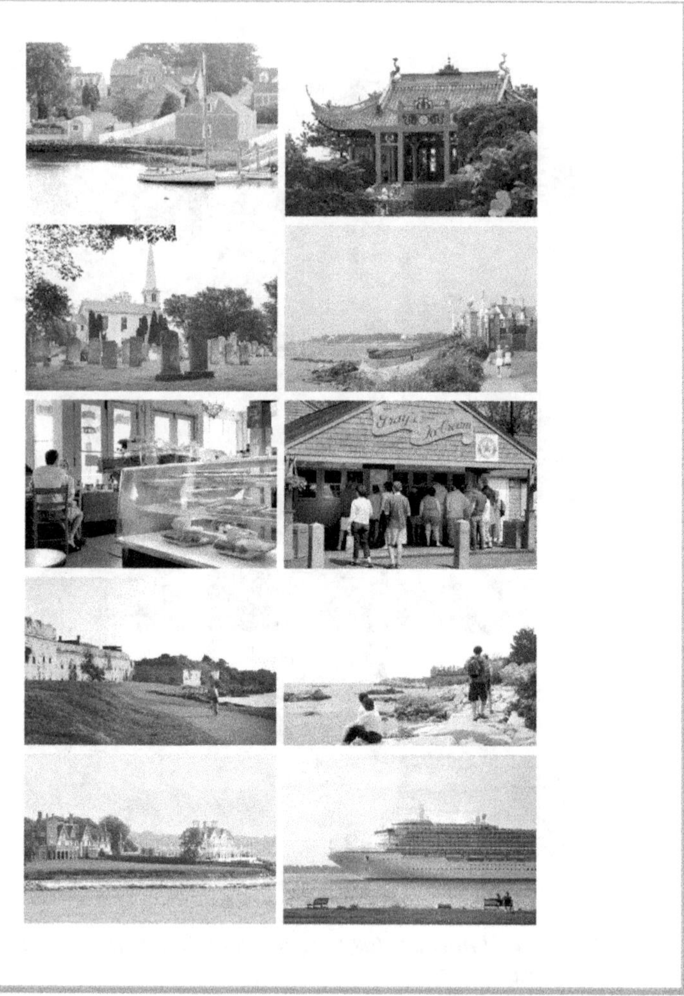

Once you have sold a few photo packages and have some quality clips, you will want to create your query material and mail it out well ahead of your vacation with the hope to get an assignment to cover the area where you will vacation.

Once established with a few publications you will send your query letters by email.

Assignments

Once you receive an assignment, you can email various museums and attractions and tell the public relations or media relations directors that you will be covering their area and ask for permission to photograph before your visit. This can lead to better access, better photos, and to interviews with the experts for detailed captioning, quotes, and material for a full article.

Just remember to dress like a professional and conduct yourself in like manner. You will be representing the publication that assigned the work and if you want to cultivate repeat assignments you must not embarrass the editor.

Research your subject before visiting so that you can plan better your photos. Look at photos of the subject on the web stock agencies and plan how your photo coverage can be different, fresh, and innovative. Make notes of important photos to take.

If you are interviewing, do prior research so that you can ask questions that will gain deeper insight into the subject without boring the interviewee. Make notes beforehand of interview questions. Use a tape recorder for quotes.

Work on Speculation

When you first start out you will want to build a clip file. You can do this if you work on self-assigned projects and cover areas where you vacation.

If you intend to cover an area as a self-assigned speculative article (you make photos without an assignment) you can still contact the PR people at those attractions and ask permission to make photos. Their level of enthusiasm will vary, but usually the State and regional tourist bureaus will be happy to send you a media packet and will be helpful. A professional approach, patience, and persistence are the keys: dress professionally, show up for appointments on time, do advance research.

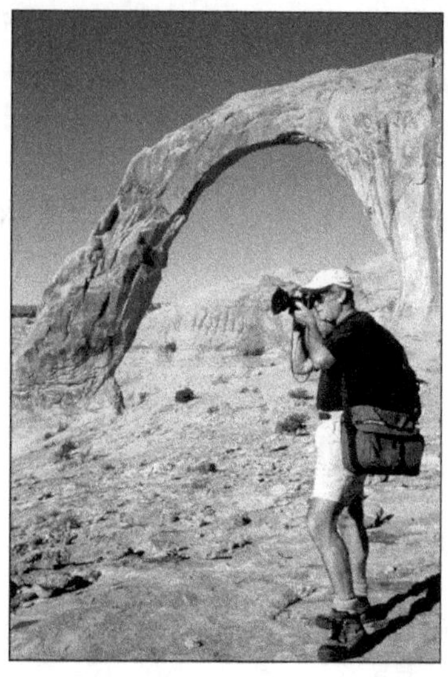

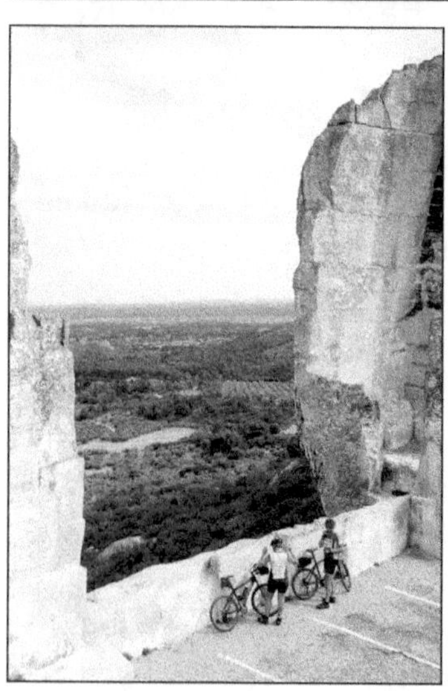

Your photos will put a slant on the travel experience. Hiking, biking dining, leisure, or romance; you tell the travel story.

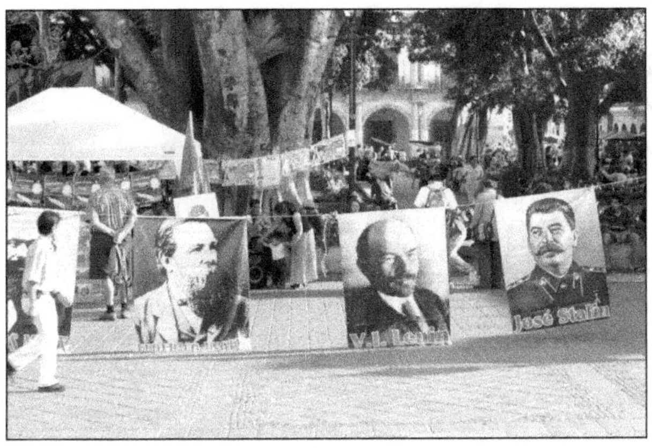

Political unrest in a country can be a travel subject for certain magazines. A study of the magazine will reveal their interest in such coverage

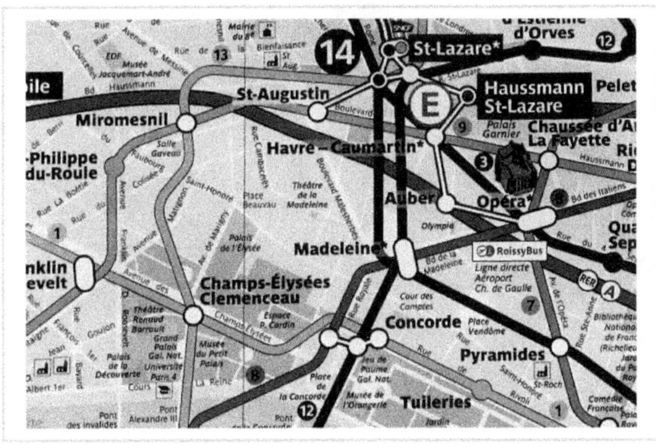

Photograph maps to get street and place names correct. Accurate captioning will include correct spelling and will become part of your reputation as a photographer.

Study The Markets

A study of the magazine will tell you which photos would be appropriate: sports, leisure, dining, biking, shopping.

Study the covers to see how much room to leave for titles and mailing labels. Design your vertical photos with the cover in mind. Include a selection of vertical photos in your offering to the editor and you will give the editor options in laying out the magazine and the option of using one of your vertical photos for the higher paying cover photo.

In the next chapter we will look at your first assignment.

In 1880, twenty four year old George Eastman opened the Eastman Dry Plate Co. in Rochester, New York. In 1888 he created flexible film and offered the first Kodak cameras loaded with enough roll film for 100 exposures. These were designed to be returned to the company for processing, printing, and reloading with film.

In 1890 Eastman made photography available to every traveler when he introduced the Kodak Brownie Box Camera.

Chapter Ten, Your First Assignment

One day an email shows up in your inbox and it is from an editor. If it comes in by paper mail, not in your self-addressed, stamped envelope but in the publisher's stationary, it is not another rejection, you have received an assignment.

Now you must deliver what you promised in your query letter, let's hope that you didn't promise too much.

The editor, in an email, will tell you what the publication wants and might expand on the photographer's guidelines. Follow the photographer's guidelines closely and package your digital photos sent via email as an attachment, burned to a CD and sent through the mail, or sent via the editors FTP line. (file transfer protocol). The delivery method will depend on what the editor requests.

If you follow directions closely, you make it easy for the editor to work with you and you will cultivate repeat assignments.

Prepare The Images For An Editor

When you start preparing images to send to an editor for an assignment you don't want to find that you can not meet the photographer's guidelines because you have made the images too small, or created them at too low a resolution, or created your images in the wrong color space. These points were covered in Chapter Six with the discussion of raw capture and will be reviewed here with the aim of sending photos to an editor.

Color Space, File Format

Color space, file size, and file format are covered in detail in the Universal Photographic Digital Imaging Guidelines, UPDIG, mentioned earlier.

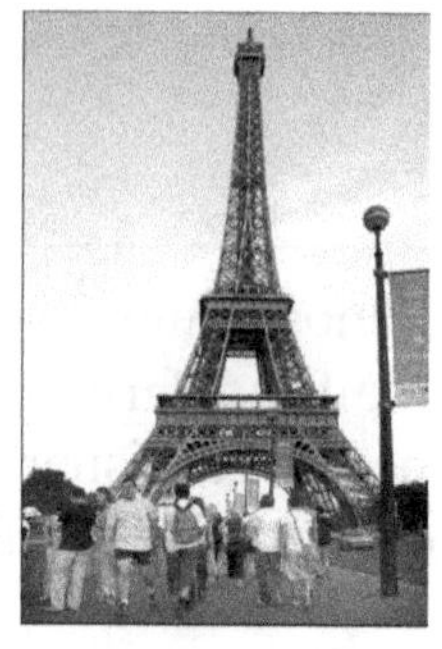

Make your verticals as files large enough for the editor to consider them as covers.

UPDIG

Check the latest on UPDIG because digital imaging is changing rapidly and much confusion for editors and print houses has resulted. The guidelines have attempted to standardize the creating, archiving, and transporting of images. *www.updig.org free download for latest guidelines*

These guidelines give detailed descriptions of color space, file type, calibration, and other related info.

While you refer to the latest UPDIG guidelines when preparing images you hope that the editors and print houses are following the same guidelines.

If you have created your photos in the Adobe RGB color space, (Ch 6) you then need only concern yourself with two file systems commonly used to store and transport images: TIFF and JPEG.

TIFF And Jpeg

TIFF stands for tagged image file format, a system developed by Aldus Co. to manage images. The developer designed the system to be usable by a broad range of devices and various brands of digital instruments. TIFF, therefore, is a popular method of working on and transporting images. Many editors will want to receive images in TIFF format because regardless of their use of Mac or PC, they will be able to open the files and do considerable work with the TIFF files.

JPEG

JPEG is another format for sending images. JPEG stands for Joint Photographic Experts Group, a consortium of industry experts that formed to devise a system of sending images over phone lines from computer to computer. JPEG file sizes will be much smaller than TIFF files and therefore will contain less information. This translates into reduced detail in dark and light areas of the image and less-gradual color transition.

Jpeg has become a common requests by photo editors, however; therefore if you do send JPEG images, you should save them at the highest quality.

Be careful with JPEGs, however; do your adjusting, levels, curves, and other corrections on the image as a 16-bit TIFF file and then convert to JPEG as a last step; don't continually JPEG an image.

To put it simply, think of TIFF as the format for working on an image while JPEG is the format for sending an image.

File Size Minimum

File size is extremely important and though touched on earlier (Ch. 6) will be covered here in more detail.

File size will be particularly important if you want to have a chance at a high-paying cover. Always capture as large a file as possible and capture in raw mode if possible or in the highest jpeg mode offered by your camera.

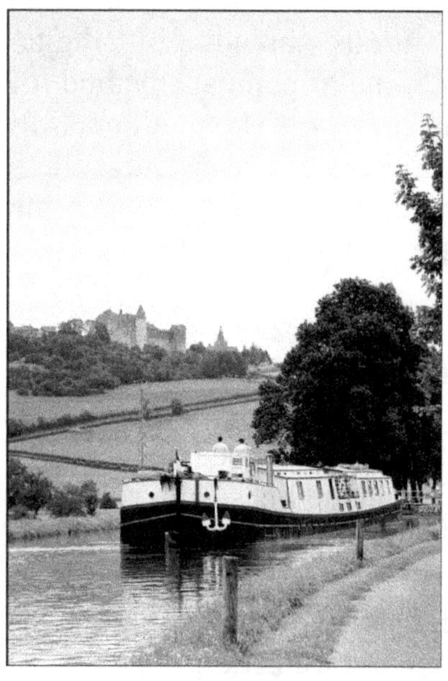

A vertical image will have cover potential and should have space at the top and bottom for the introduction of text and the mailing label.

The files should be sized to 13 inches by 19 inches by 300 dpi/ppi and sent to the editor or agency as a TIFF or jpeg.

At this size the file should be adequate for any application.

The film-based photographer scanning slides or negatives should do the scanning at a high resolution of at least 4,000 dpi/ppi at 100% for a slide or 35 mm negative, in order to yield a large enough file for enlargement to a cover.

Cover

A cover shot in a glossy magazine can bring you $300 and up; you will want to make sure that you can deliver a file large enough for enlargement to a cover. You will likely send your vertical images sized to 13x19 inches at 300 ppi, TIFF unless otherwise directed by the editor.

With a cover in mind you can send vertical images that have cover

potential as clean unsharpened files of around 40 to 60 megabytes.
This will all depend on the photographer's guidelines and instructions from the photo editor.

Preparing Images For Sending To An Editor

As mentioned in Chapter 6 you should capture your digital photographs in raw mode if possible. This will create a 12 or 16-bit file that will better reproduce detail in shadows and highlights. Save the raw file just as it is. These unaltered files become your archive. From a copy of this raw file you prepare images for sending to the editor.

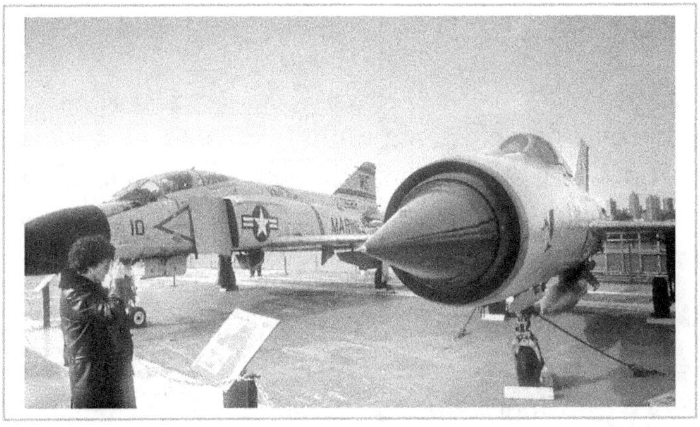

When making photos while on vacation, include people in your composition to make a more marketable product. It is best to offer model-released photos. This will give the photo more value and increase the photo's sales potential. Take both horizontal and vertical photos to give yourself a chance at a cover, a full page, or double-page spread.
In a museum setting such as that above, make contact beforehand with the PR Director and ask for a property release

First convert the copy of the raw file to a TIFF file using the software that came with the camera or another imaging program. Disable sharpening or set it to zero in the software when you do the conversion.

Next, perform the levels and curves, color balance, and other tweaking changes that you deem necessary. Don't alter the image excessively. (Be sure here that your computer monitor is calibrated if you will perform color corrections, Chapter 6)

Some programs will allow you to work on a 16-bit image to retain subtlety and you should do this if possible. After making adjustments in 16-bit, reduce the image to 8-bit as a last step. It is often easier and faster, however, to work on an 8-bit image and, for less stringent publication such as newspapers, an 8-bit image will be adequate.

Dust

Tiny dust particles on a digital camera's sensor and on the front and back lens element of a DSLR with interchangeable lenses can leave round dark areas on an image that will show up when you inspect the image at 100%. Usually dust is prominent in the sky or in large areas of a single color.

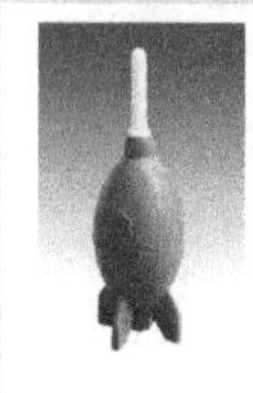

Empty your camera bag occasionally and clean out the dust.

Each time you use the digital SLR with interchangeable lenses, you might need to clean the sensor and the front and back element of the lens. This can be done with the tool pictured left which, with a squeeze of the bulb, forces air over the sensor or lens element to remove dust. Squeeze the bulb a few times to clean it before you use it on the sensor.

Do not use canned compressed air to clean the sensor because this could cause damage to your sensor.

Sensor swabs are also available to remove stubborn dust particles.

Photographic Solutions Inc. makes a variety of swabs. www.photosol.com

If spots do show up on your image, you can remove them with the cloning tool in imaging software.

If you are scanning slides you will also need to clean dust from the slides with compressed air before scanning.

Use caution when using a scanner's automatic dust removal software as it can decrease the sharpness of an image. It is best to test the dust removal software first and compare the results at 100 % on the computer monitor.

File Size

An image file could start in the digital camera as an 8-megabyte raw file and then open to a 24 megabyte TIFF depending on the camera and the software used to convert the image.

Editors of stock agencies and magazines want large files, up to 60 megabytes approximately, or a file large enough to yield a 13x19 inch image at 300 dots per inch.

Your 12+ megapixel camera will make these large files but if you must increase the file size of a digital image, stock agencies recommend software called Genuine Fractals or they recommend Adobe Photoshop, Version Seven and higher, for its interpolation system in image sizing. While interpolation can upsize an image, the programs do have limited ability; you must start with a large, unsharpened file.

Film based photographers should scan slides or 35 mm negatives at 4000 dpi (minimum, optical) at 100 % to get a file around 60 megabytes in size.

The editor will tell you in a letter or in the photographer's guidelines just what size the images should be and how to send them. Requests vary greatly. Some editors prefer digital files while others prefer slides in slide pages and medium and large format transparencies with accompanying captions. Publications vary.

Once you have your 16-bit, TIFF file sized and ready, perform an inspection at 100%, (Ctrl-Alt-0, PC Photoshop) and remove any dust spots that might have been on your sensor or lenses.

You will then send the images to the editor as unsharpened, 16-bit TIFF files if you will send your photos by CD, or you will send them via modem/FTP or you will convert them to the highest quality 8-bit JPEG and send them by email or via the editors FTP line. This will depend on the editor's directions.

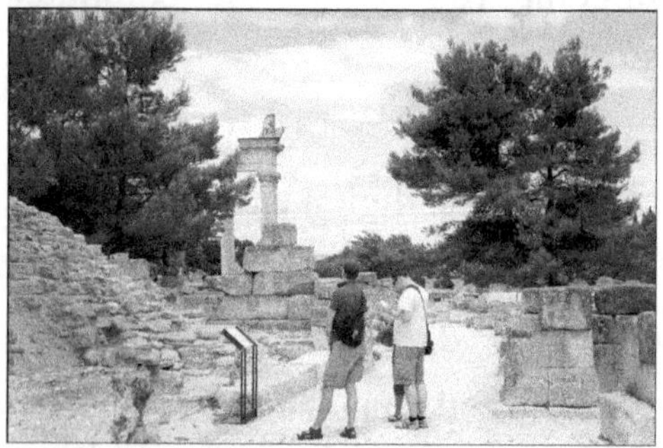

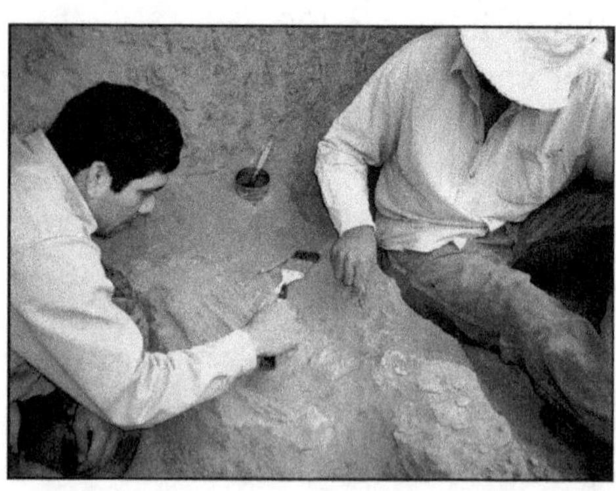

People interest the readers of travel magazines. Editors want people in your photos.

After you have delivered a few packages for publication, you will have a better understanding of which publications do a thorough job of preparing images for printing and which ones do not. You can then, in the absence of the publication's pre-press preparation, do a little more of your own, particularly in saturation if they are using an uncoated paper like newsprint. You can also apply a last-step, unsharp mask if they do not routinely sharpen.

Rights

Once you have received the assignment you then must agree on the terms.

The editor has accepted your proposal and now you will face the issues of rights: under what conditions and at what price will you supply photos to the editor.

The editor will spell out the rights they would like to buy. There are several ways you can grant rights to use your creative material; most common are: "One Time Rights." and, "First North American Serial Rights." The photographer's guidelines that you receive from the editor might list the rights that the publication will buy. If not in the guidelines, the rights will be in a contract.

Rights asked by various publications will differ.

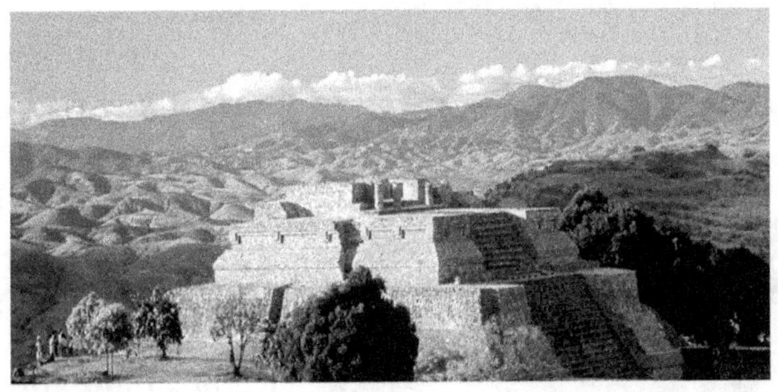

Monte Alban, a monumental city built by South Central Mexico's Zapotec culture in 500 BC

Usually you will offer One Time Rights with a photo like this and grant the publication rights to run it in one issue of a monthly magazine to illustrate a text article. If you sold all rights you could not use this image again.

One-Time Rights

One-time rights give the publisher permission to use your photo in one issue of the magazine, something akin to renting the image. You retain ownership of the work and can offer it to others. To cultivate repeat sales with that editor, however, you should not offer the same image to competing magazines within the same year.

First North American Serial Rights

Under this contract, you grant the editor the right to use your photos for the first time in North America and for a specified time (90 days) before you will offer it to any other publication in North America. You can offer the work in other countries at the same time

All Rights

Some publications request all rights, meaning that they want to own the image. Exercise caution with a publication that requests all rights, you could give away any future rights to sell use of that image.

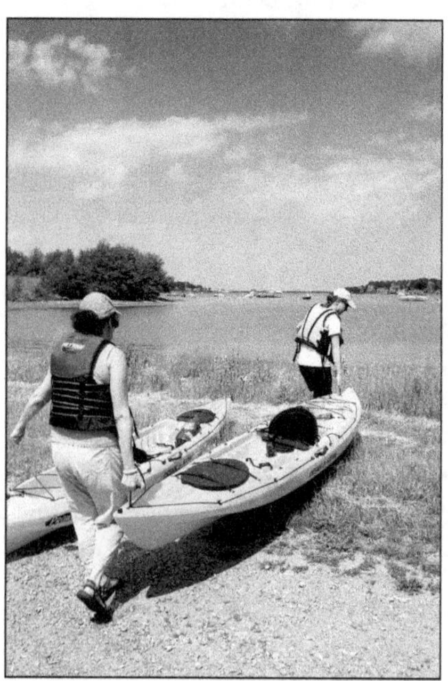

Unusual images can sell many times for you so it is best to offer your images for One-Time use or offer First North American Serial Rights, until you have a firmer grasp of the business side of marketing photos and a better understanding of the value of your images.

Send Files

You can send files in several ways. It will depend on the editor's request.

One method is to send files burned to a CD as 8 or 16-bit TIFF files. In that format the editors will be able to open the files regardless of the type of computer that they use and they will be able to do extensive work on the images.

If you send by CD, check to see that your CD burner is set to ISO 9660 or a system that both PC and Mac can read before burning. Create the discs at the slowest write speed available to avoid errors. Check your results after burning by opening the files yourself before you send the disc to the editor.

Another method is to send images as an attachment to an email. This is less costly and time consuming for both you and the editor but will limit the file size.

Another method is the FTP line (file transfer protocol) similar to uploading images to a website. It will depend on the editor's request.

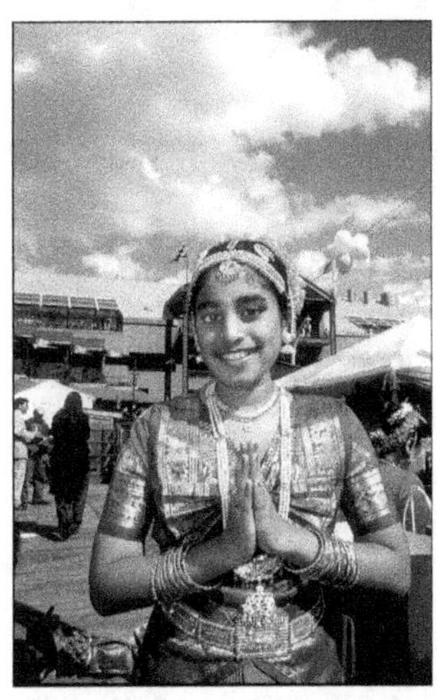

Cultural festival can yield interesting travel photos.

Manuscript

If you are sending a manuscript, you can also send that by CD or in an email. Manuscripts and caption pages sent via email are best attached as a PDF file to avoid data loss. (Portable Document Format) PDF.

(Download a free PDF writer if you don't have this program)

Some publications still request paper or hard copy manuscripts: a double-spaced printed text in New Times

Roman at font size 12 for instance, but most magazines and trade papers do not require a paper manuscript. They want the text and photo captions on disc or in an email PDF.

Although the computer has made creating a manuscript easier than ever, do not rely too heavily on your computer's spell check. Use it wisely but also proof read or have a proofreader check your work.

Read your query letter, manuscript, and captions aloud to see how they flow and to pick up errors.

If you are sending images or text to an editor via email, it is a good practice to send one to yourself with the attached images before you send it to the editor to make sure that you can open the text and the images.

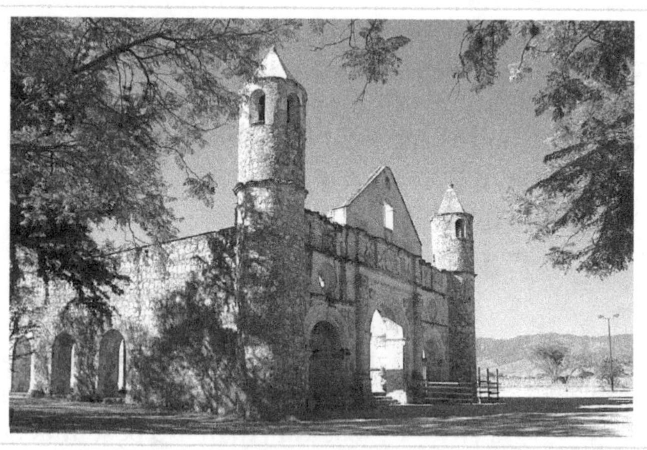

The Ex-Convento of Cuilapan, a Dominican church built in 1555 in Oaxaca Mexico to convert the indigenous Zapotec and Mixtec population living three hundred miles south of Mexico City to Christianity.
A caption should tell the Who, What, When, Where, and Why.

Label

Be sure to label everything that you send. You can write on the disc with a CD marker, printing your name, phone number, email address, and the title of the photo feature. Do not put paper labels on CDs, however, because they can make the CD unstable during reading.

Include Metadata

Metadata is the information that accompanies a digital image: time when taken, camera model, exposure, ISO, etc. Keep the metadata on your digital images intact. Be sure that your camera's clock and date information are accurate so that the editor can be clear on when the photos were made. This data can include your copyright info and contact information. Place the copyright info in the metadata with your camera software or other imaging program.

Label everything and include your contact info.

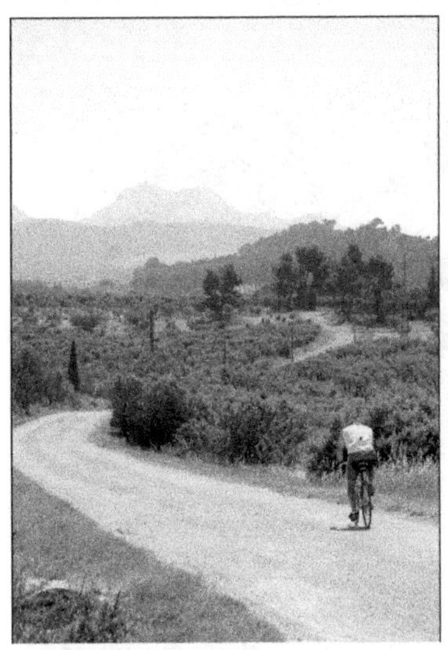

Create the feeling of freedom in your text and photos. Set up the camera at a place with an s-curve on a country road and wait for people enjoying a hike or bike ride to fill your frame.

Captions

Lucid captioning of photos is crucial and should tell the, who, what, when, where, why, and how of the photos on a separate printed page and in a text within the file contained on the CD or in a text file in a PDF attached to an email. Send reference thumbnails with caption numbers so that the editor can match the caption to the photo.

More About Photographer's Guidelines

Photographer's guidelines can vary greatly from various editors and often they need updating because digital imaging is rapidly changing the way publications work.

If the editor does not spell out just how you will deliver your images, you can request the latest guides with an email and clarify any questions about how to send your images.

In the absence of clear guides, send TIFF images sized to 8 x 12 inches at 300 ppi and burned to a CD. Email to alert the editor that you have sent the assignment. Otherwise make the same size files converted at the highest quality to jpeg and sent via DSL, cable modem, or wireless as an attachment to an email with caption info in a PDF file.

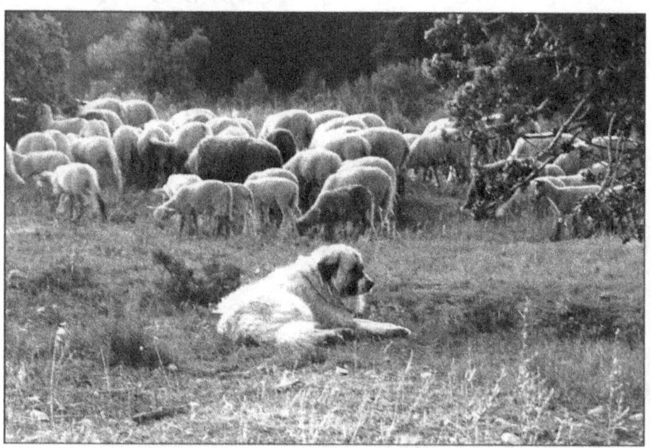

Capture the icons of the place and capture in raw or the highest Jpeg that your camera can make so that your photos will be open to a variety of markets.

Terms

The photographer's guidelines or the contract that you agree to with the publication should list the terms of payment and all other information. An assignment should specify clearly what the proposal will pay and when you deliver, your deadline.

Some editors will ask you to invoice them. This is a good practice so that you receive the agreed on amount.

Save all correspondence with the editor, both letter and email. A year or more could elapse between the time you receive an assignment and the time the publication uses your photos. In the intervening months the editor might leave the publication. You are still under contract to deliver the photos and the publication is obligated to pay you for your work. Your emails and letters document the transaction.

For reasons of documentation, ask editors who like to assign via a phone conversation to send the assignment in an email. The email will be your record of the assignment.

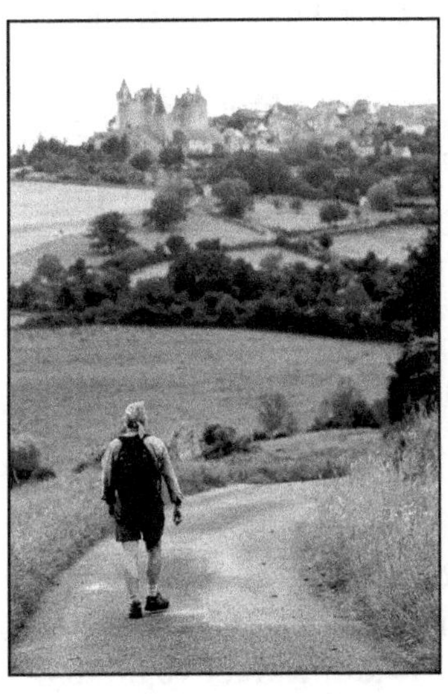

Find the s-curve and set up the tripod. Set your camera to RGB capture 100 ISO manual mode. Read the light meter in the foreground, mid-ground, and background. Attach a GND if needed and a lens shade. Pre-focus the lens and set the exposure. Now wait for someone enjoying a travel activity to fill your landscape for a sense of place photo that tells the travel story: Hiking in the Burgundy Valley, France.

Send CD Or Email

Follow the editor's request.

If you do have options, however, the easiest and least expensive way for you to send photos and caption text is via email as PDF files. If the editor offers an FTP, you will have another low-cost way to send them.

(Filezilla, FirefTP, WinSCP, Cyberduck and ClassicFTP are some typical FTP sites)

You might also send them on a CD. The CD, however, will include some expense on your part for the CD, the cover, packaging, and postage.
Since you will have copies of this CD you don't need to insure the shipment, and you don't need a return of the material.

Provided that the files are sent as the editor requested, they should not be limited in how large they can make your photos. As TIFF files on CD or PDF files and JPEG via the web, any editor using PC or Mac should be able to open your files.

Send a cover letter with your CD, reminding the editor of the assignment and describing the contents of the CD.

Cultivate Repeat Assignments
The best way to get work and to get repeat work is to make it easy for the editor to work with you.

Meet the deadline or alert the editor as quickly as possible if you can not meet the deadline. Above all, try to deliver your best and most appropriate photos, detailed and accurate captions, and photos sized to the editor's request.

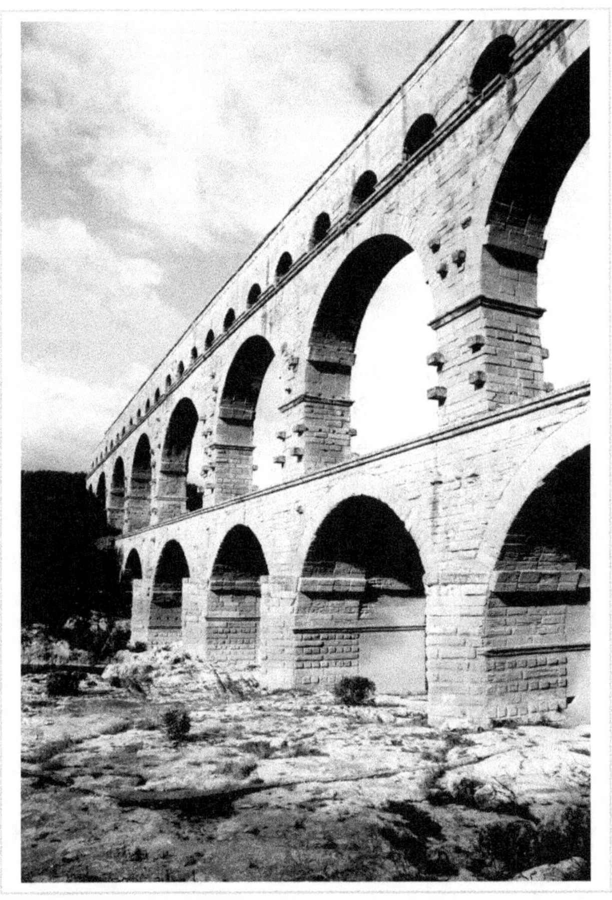

Pont Du Gard, France, a Roman-built aqueduct near Nimes
This photo provides space at the top and bottom for logos and mailing labels and other supporting text.

Reference Books:
(A classic) Sell & Re-Sell Your Photos by Rohn Engh
Noted for its emphasis on stock photography
Photography Outdoors: A Field Guide For Travel and Adventure Photographers, by Art Wolfe and Mark Gardner

John Shaw's Landscape Photography, by John Shaw

Complete Digital Photography, by Ben Long
A five star text book on digital camera photography
Digital Photography Book by Scott Kelby

Photo Equipment Suppliers:
B&H Photo and Video, 420 Ninth Avenue, New York, NY 10001 www.bhphotovideo.com 1-800-947-9978
A huge retail store in New York City and a mail order dealer with good quality and good prices.

Web Sites:
Research Digital Equipment, www.stevesgdigicam.com

www.NYIP.com/ezine/ good info, instruction

http://digital-photography-school.com/author/darren web photo instruction
www.MondoTimes.co listing of thousands of trade publications

www.Adobe.com/digitalimag/AdobeRGB.html

www.photographersmarket.com Listings of editors and publications that buy rights to publish photos and articles.

www.updig.org Free Download of imaging standards

http://kropla.com/electric2.htm World wide electrical plug configurations.

In 1982, Sony introduced the Mavica, a still video camera capturing images on a computer disk.
By 2004 Kodak had announced the end of film camera production in the US. In 2006 Canon announced that it would no longer manufacture film cameras.

Now It Is Your Turn

There may be no better feeling for you as a photographer than to walk into a book store and see a travel photo that you created on the cover of a magazine. Follow the steps in this book and it will happen.

Although many details remain, this quick-start tutorial should put you on the fast track to selling your travel photos. Above all be honest, keep it simple, and be patient; you will sell if you send out enough proposals and keep honing your photo technique with the aim of filling a photo editor's needs.

Anticipate The Editor's Needs

An understanding of those photo editor's needs is your key; read the photo guidelines and study the magazine and stock agency requests. Fill the editors needs and make it easy for them to work with you by maintaining a consistently professional manner and you will sell.

New websites and agencies frequently come to the market looking for fresh material. Once you find your niche, you will have repeat sales and take delight in seeing your images in publication.

We wish you success.

Glossary of Terms

Aperture: *The opening in the lens that regulates the amount of light reaching the film plane or digital sensor. This is calibrated in numbers: f-32, f-22, f-16, f-11, f-8, f-5.6, f-4*

Artifact: *an unwanted distortion in an image usually caused by a low quality compression such as a Jpeg done at low quality or Jpeging an image repeatedly*

Bit: *Short for binary Digit, the smallest unit of computer memory; 8 bits comprise a byte; a thousand bytes make a kilobyte.*

Bulb: *The setting on a camera that allows a infinitely long exposure.*

Burn CD: *storing information on a CD, so called because a laser burns the information into the disc.*

Color Model: *commonly called color space and usually referring to RGB, CYMK, and sRGB. The color systems that digital equipment commonly use.*

Compression: *storing images in a file format that decreases file size. Some compression systems like Jpeg result in the loss of some information, others like TIFF are lossless.*

Digital: *Any material done on a computer*

Digital Zoom: *The apparent zooming in of a lens but in reality a zooming done digitally by cropping in the camera. This is not an actual optical zooming. Digital zooming will most often produce unsatisfactory images for publication.*

DPI: *Dots per inch, a measure of the density of dots of color or information in a digital print*

DSL: *Digital Subscriber Line, a common computer telephone system for sending images and text.*

Exposure: *the amount of light reaching the film or digital sensors, determined by shutter speed and aperture settings on the camera*

***F Stop**: number assigned to the opening of the adjustable aperture which controls the amount of light entering the camera.*

***FTP, File Transfer Protocol:** A method of sending files from a computer to a server in a distant place or to another country. The server could be in the publishing house*

***Gamut**: The range of colors that a device can capture or display*

***Graduated Neutral Density Filter**: A filter that will darken a portion of the lens to prevent over exposure and help balance the exposure.*

***Interpolation**: Refers to an upsizing of an image by creating new pixels based on the information in the existing pixels of an image.*

***ISO:** International Standards Organization, referring to film speed and digital capture speed ratings. Formerly called ASA, the 50 to 100 range is considered slow and without grain or digital noise. The 400 speed can be noisy or grainy. For publication, use 100 ISO or less.*

***JPEG**: An image compression system that discards some information when reducing the size of a file. A preferred method for sending images over a modem or phone line or for the web (Joint Photographic Experts Group)*

***Lens**: A glass device on the camera commonly classed by focal length or length from front element of the lens to the film or sensor plain.*

***Lens Flare:** Drastic lens flare results in octagonal light spots on an image usually caused by direct sunlight entering the lens. Subtle flare results in a reduction of contrast and occurs when stray light enters the lens. A lens shade prevents this.*

***Lens Shade**: an attachment to the front of a lens that shades the lens element from unwanted light.*

***Metadata:** Information applied by your camera to your photo. Imaging software can also apply metadata to images such as your contact info and copyright*

***Megapixel:** Millions of pixels, a term to describe the light capturing ability of a camera.*

Noise: *an unacceptable grain pattern in a digital image usually caused by high capture speed above 200 ISO, by low light, or by excessive image manipulation in the computer.*

Optical Zoom: *A true zooming in to a subject by the changing of the lens optics. An action that results in a quality zoom when compared to a digital zoom.*

Pixel: *Short for Picture element, the pixel is the building block of the digital image. Images in the computer are sized by the number of pixels per inch, PPI .*

PPI: *the number of pixels per inch in an image, a measure of its resolution. The higher the number of PPI in an image, the higher the resolution, and usually, the higher the quality of the image. Incorrectly used interchangeably with dpi, dots per inch, a term that refers to printer resolution.*

Resolution: *refers usually to the number of pixels per inch of an image, commonly the determining factor in the quality or printability of an image. For convenience, editors of publications use the minimum of 300 pixels per inch, PPI. Editors might use dots per inch, DPI and pixels per inch interchangeably in their communications.*

Stops: *The opening of the lens aperture is calibrated in stops of light called f-stops. f-4, f-5.6, f-8, f-11 and so on to f-27 or f-32.*

TIFF: *Tagged Image File Format, an image file system usable by both Mac and PC computer systems for managing images. Recommended along with Jpeg as a method of delivering images to magazine or stock photo editors.*

White Balance: *A feature found in the menu of a digital camera that will change the color of artificial light and make it look like daylight. You can set this in the camera to occur automatically.*

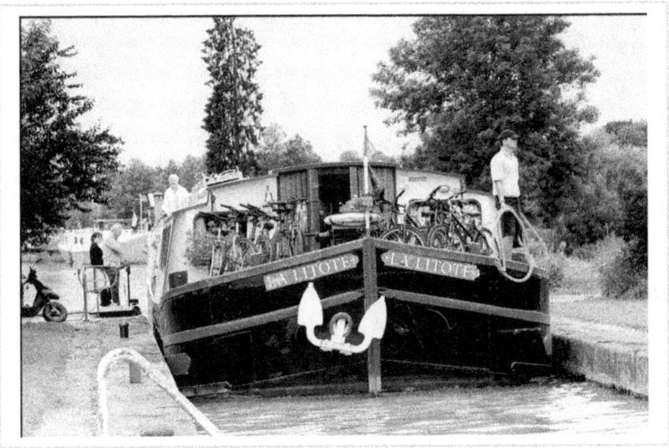

Canal Barge locking through on the Burgundy Canal, France

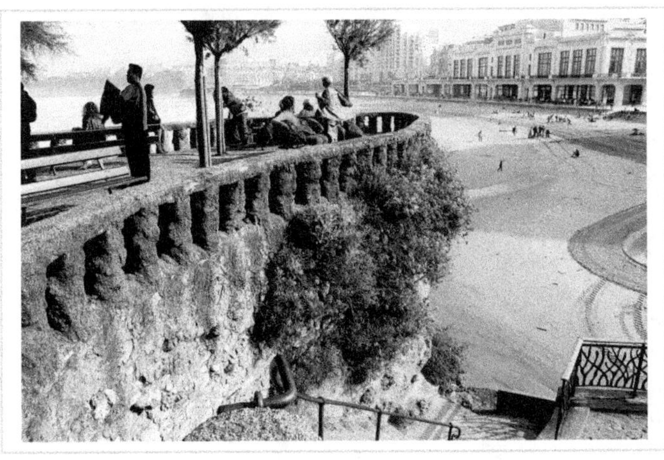

Bairritz, a beach town on the Atlantic in Southwestern France is noted for luxury resorts, casino gambling, golf, and surfing

Index

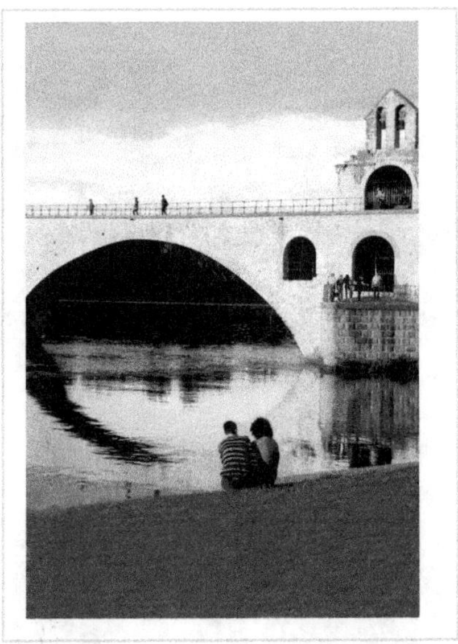

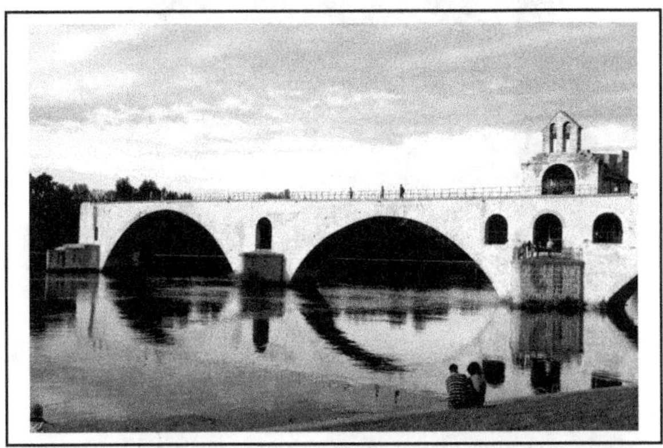

Send verticals and horizontals (portrait mode and landscape mode) to give the editor choices.

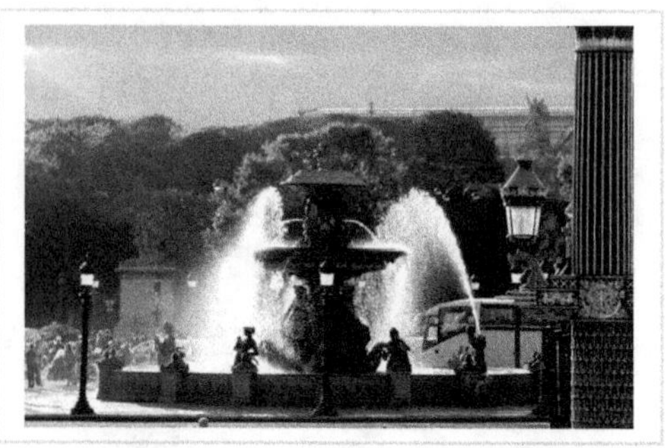

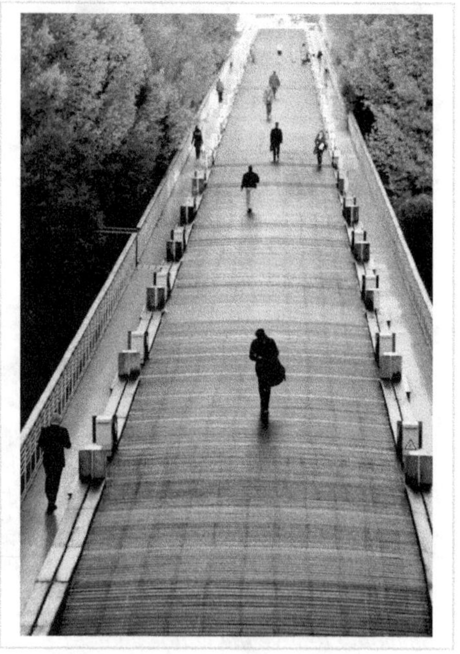

Send the editor choices of both vertical and horizontal photos

www.ingramcontent.com/pod-product-compliance
Lightning Source LLC
Chambersburg PA
CBHW060854170526
45158CB00001B/347